THE REFERENCE SHELF (Continued)

THE REFERENCE SHELF

Vol. 28   No. 6

THE MIDDLE EAST
IN THE COLD WAR

Edited by
GRANT S. McCLELLAN

THE H. W. WILSON COMPANY
NEW YORK   1956

PREFACE

One author on the Middle East has called it the "world without end." And rightly, for it was the scene where some of the first civilizations began and where others also rose, and fell, over long centuries. Time seems to stretch unendingly into the future, too, for the vast majority of the peoples of the area—time in which the lot of those many millions will apparently change but little from patterns of life centuries old.

But the Middle East is also a "new" area and is now undergoing stepped-up change which has been induced by both internal and external pressures. Needless to say the Middle East, like other vitally strategic areas, has been caught up in the striking and often violent changes that have occurred so generally in the wake of World War II. If the older British and French stakes in the area have diminished or been abandoned, both the United States and the Soviet Union have from the end of the war taken renewed interest in all of the Arab lands, in Israel, Turkey, Iran and Pakistan. (The North African Arab areas are not dealt with in this book.) New states have been created in the area and colonial rule or protection has all but ceased to exist. Obviously the emergence of Israel with all of the complexities inherent in its founding and survival has opened up many critical new factors. From the first the Middle East was also a crucial spot in the Cold War between East and West. The handling of the area's most important natural resource, aside from its peoples, has also taken a new, if not clearly defined, turn since the war. Following the postwar Anglo-Iranian dispute over the rich Iranian oil deposits, all of the area's foreign petroleum operations have, in effect, been alerted to prospective change.

The Middle East is also new in that broader and deeper currents of thought and action, which are at work for the first time, are now becoming more clearly revealed. In the long vistas of history which characterize the Middle East, it is permissible to refer to events within a mere century as recent. In these terms some areas have had nodding acquaintance with at least the forms of democracy for nearly a hundred years. More recently, many leadership groups have begun to reexamine the attempts that have been made to transplant democracy to their homelands. The reappraisal has led to disillusionment in some cases and even to abandoning the democratic way. Communism as a creed has also entered the scene and has had a definite appeal, though mainly among the intelligentsia. Meanwhile certain leaders of Islam, the predominant religion of the area, have emerged to champion reactionary trends within their creed. Also some of the present political leaders have veered quite definitely of late toward neutralism in world affairs.

Finally, recent events in the East-West struggle give to the Middle East a new look that it has not had since World War II. As the Cold War has changed in the post-Stalin period, the Middle East has seen the entrance of the Soviet Union on the spot in a way that Russia's long drive toward the area, dating from the pre-Communist era of the Czars, never achieved. With the sale of Soviet-bloc arms to Egypt and Russian offers of economic and technical aid to several countries in the Middle East, a distinctly new situation has arisen. In the early Cold War years, the United States and the free world resisted Soviet attempts to penetrate the area both in Iran and in Greece; such efforts eventually culminated in the organization of defense for the northern countries under the 1955 Baghdad Pact. It is this barrier on the "northern tier" which has been vaulted by the new Soviet tactics. And in mid-1956 a new crisis was precipitated when Egypt retaliated against the West by nationalizing the Suez Canal after the United States and Britain had withdrawn their offer to help Egypt build the High Aswan Dam.

What all of these changes portend cannot, of course, yet be determined. These changes and other thorny problems appear like unknowns in an equation. But it is over these questions and situations as well as the more general way in which the Middle East is involved in world affairs that this book ranges. Necessarily it can touch upon many topics only briefly.

A previous Reference Shelf book—*Crisis in the Middle East* (Volume 24, Number 4), edited by Edward Latham—dealt with the area at the beginning of 1952. That book and its bibliography should be consulted in connection with the present one. Many of the controversial issues arising in the area are discussed in both books. The materials here attempt to bring the fascinating and complex story of the Middle East up to date. They tend also to reveal some of the realities of the situation which have become clearer as the Great Power struggle over the Middle East and the tensions within have mounted.

Because there is so much controversy about the Middle East, it should be emphasized that the articles compiled here do not necessarily reflect the views of either the editor or publisher. The editor, however, gratefully acknowledges the permission to reprint the selections which follow. He is also indebted to Miss Betty Davey for assistance in preparing this compilation.

GRANT S. MCCLELLAN

September 18 1956

CONTENTS

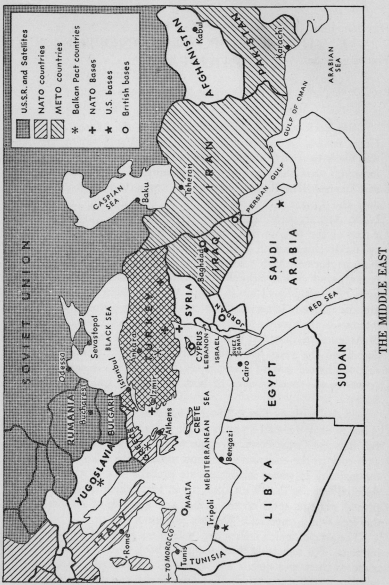

THE MIDDLE EAST

Adapted from "The Middle East Today" pamphlet by Emil Lengyel. (Discussion Series no 2)
Foreign Policy Association. New York. 1954. p32-3.

I. THE GREAT POWERS AND THE MIDDLE EAST

EDITOR'S INTRODUCTION

This book leads off with a discussion of the interests of the Great Powers in the Middle East. The struggle among them over the area is an old one. It has now taken on new forms, new meanings, and there are new participants. France is definitely still interested in the area though it was ousted from its hold over the Levant states during World War II. Its interest in North African lands, whose independence is now championed by Arabs of the Middle East, means that France must keep a keen eye on developments in the area. The influence and ties of Britain with its former Arab friends have been tested in the extreme recently and many traditional British commitments in the area have been abandoned since World War II. New to the scene are the United States and the Soviet Union. Not that their interests in the area do not have long historical precedents. Those of America are discussed more fully in Section V; those of Russia date from the years when the Czars dreamed of pushing their rule southward toward warm water ports. What is new is the active, on-the-spot activities of both the Soviets and the United States.

To deal with the Great Power struggle in the Middle East first is not to deny the vital interests of the states within the area itself. But it is the Great Power struggle which remains most dramatic as it may in the end prove the most violent. At stake is an area the majority of whose inhabitants are probably not yet committed definitely in the East-West conflict; an area which is one of the pivotal strategic spots on the globe; and a source of oil vital to the free world, especially Western Europe.

The articles which follow deal with these general Great Power interests. But inevitably throughout the book further reference is made to them and details are unfolded, for example, about the problem of oil in the Middle East; the British and the question of

Cyprus; Soviet support of the growing arms race between Israel and the Arab states; American attempts to construct a defense line on Russia's southern borders; and others. So complex are the problems of the area that Great Power and local political, economic, social and military issues are closely interwoven. The articles immediately following, therefore, take on further significance as those of the later portions of the book are related to them.

The first article, by a student of the area, sets forth briefly many factors that are discussed throughout the book. The next article states what the official commitments of the Great Powers in the area are. But it should be remembered that private, semi-governmental and other government commitments exist in the sense that American, British and French (among other) firms and governments also have special interests in petroleum operations, the Suez Canal and military bases in the area. The most recent development in which the Anglo-American powers have taken part by further committing themselves to the defense of the region is discussed in connection with the Baghdad Pact (which set up the Middle East Treaty Organization). Both British and United States interests, the first on the decline and the latter on the rise, are explained in the next two articles. One interpretation of Soviet designs on the area is then presented. The next article, critical of the Baghdad Pact, is also critical of American policy, but it suggests some of the unfortunate possible consequences of the present Great Power struggle in the area as it shapes up with the active part Soviet Russia is now playing on the actual scene. The last two articles comment on the strategic and economic importance of the Suez Canal and on the negotiations over the crisis which arose in mid-1956.

THE "NEW" MIDDLE EAST [1]

Among the more notable developments in international affairs during recent years are two which, taken together, give considerable character to the contemporary international scene. One is

[1] From "The Quest for Security in the Middle East," by Halford L. Hoskins, senior specialist in international relations of the Library of Congress. *Annals of the American Academy of Political and Social Science.* 294:138-46. July 1954. Reprinted by permission.

the evolution of what may be called a "new" Middle East. The other is the rapid growth of interest in the countries comprising this area on the part of the United States. . . .

If we apply the expression "Middle East" to the lands adjacent to the eastern end of the Mediterranean Sea and extending thence to the borders of the subcontinent of India, we are referring, from the point of view of human culture, to the oldest countries in the world. Yet in several ways they are now to be counted among the youngest. Their newness is not to be measured by the elapsed time since they achieved independent status, even though this interval has been brief in every instance. It is rather to be gauged by the degree of maturity exhibited by their political and social institutions; by the type of judgment displayed by their political leaders in formulating and in executing public policy; by the extent to which genuine national patriotism has succeeded in uniting the various elements of the populations and in creating modern, viable nations. In terms such as these, the Middle East is young indeed, and for the most part still conspicuously immature. . . .

Except for a hard outer shell in Turkey, the countries of the Middle East must be described as essentially soft in a world—and especially in a strategic area—where softness is a constant temptation to great powers which regard aggression as a fitting instrument of state policy. "Softness" in the Middle East is the result of several contributing causes. Some of them are products of the physical environment. Not too much in terms of economic strength, political development, and material progress can be expected of a country much of whose area is inescapably arid, as in the case of Syria, the Hashemite Kingdom of Jordan, Saudi Arabia, or Iran, or mountainous, as in Lebanon or Yemen. Sudden wealth in the form of oil cannot quickly atone for the lack of other natural resources, such as arable soil, adequate rainfall, or deposits of the hard minerals of industry. Not a little of the underdeveloped character of parts of the Middle East is the result of centuries of Ottoman rule—a regime in which individual enterprise was regarded as subversive. To these factors might be added the influences of climate, age-old poverty, fatalistic philosophy, and even the external environment. For considering the position of the Middle East with reference to great power relationships, it is clear that the peoples of the area cannot hope to be left to develop their institutional life unhampered—or perhaps unhelped—by one or more of the powers whose interests are global in scope.

Barricade or Barrier

It is the position occupied by the countries of the Middle East quite as much as any intrinsic need for technical assistance or economic aid that accounts for the present interest of the United States in these underdeveloped nations. In a world where two power alignments of states are essentially at war, the Middle East forms either a barricade or a barrier to both power groups. In so far as the area serves to prevent access by the Soviet Union to the Mediterranean and the Persian Gulf—that is, to the sea lanes reaching to South Asia, southern Europe, and the greater part of the African continent—it figures as a barricade in defense plans of the free world. To the extent that it inhibits—or in time of war may inhibit—uninterrupted access of the Western powers to the southern shores of Asia, the eastern shores of Africa, and the British Commonwealth countries in Australasia, the Middle East is a potential barrier. It may well be observed, too, that the maintenance of dependable lines of free world communications through this area is not less essential in an air age than in one confined to surface travel. Even if Middle East refueling bases were not required, permission to cross national boundaries still is requisite. Few features of a strategic concept for the free world are more fundamental than maintaining a balance of influence throughout the Middle East.

Oil

The securing of lines of commercial intercourse with parts of the Middle East is not less consequential than the maintenance of other lines of communications, because of the part which petroleum plays in contemporary international relations. It is conceivable that in time to come atomic forces may in part supersede those now derived from petroleum. Meanwhile . . . oil in the contemporary world is power. . . . Any optimistic outlook for the free world, in fact, rests on the availability to the United States, as the leader of the free world, of adequate supplies of petroleum at all times and under any circumstances.

It is the greatest of good fortune, therefore, that more than one third of the world's oil resources, according to current estimates, lie within the Western Hemisphere and presumably—although not altogether certainly—will be constantly available to this country in time of peace or war. The satisfaction to which this circumstance might give rise, however, is gravely compromised by other considerations. One lies in the fact that even now, in time of relative peace and with no unusual handicaps on oil production, the United States consumes approximately two thirds of all the oil used anywhere in the world. Undoubtedly in time of all-out war it would require more.

Another major consideration consists in the oil needs of Western Europe. The North Atlantic Treaty Organization, of which the United States was one of the principal architects, was created on the assumption that the defense of Western Europe is vital to the survival of the free world in the struggle with Communist totalitarianism. In this struggle European industry is counted on heavily to supplement that of the United States and Canada. But Europe does not rank high among the oil-producing areas and must be supplied mainly from extra-European sources. Inasmuch as the necessary quantities of oil cannot be drawn from Western Hemisphere sources without overtaxing those producing fields, the responsibility for European supply since 1948 has fallen principally on the sparsely populated oil-producing countries of the Middle East, whose minimal local oil needs and slight industrial development have represented complementary rather than competing demands.

In the uninterrupted continuation of the westward flow of Middle East oil the United States thus has an extremely important interest. . . . In the interest of free institutions and possibly even its own survival, the United States faces the problem of establishing and maintaining in the Middle East conditions under which the defense of the area can be assured within reason and the flow of petroleum and petroleum products made secure under any easily imaginable circumstances.

United States and the Middle East

It cannot be said that the United States has displayed a great deal either of ambition or of aptitude for the task of making sure of the westward orientation of the nations of the Middle East. Until World War II brought this country into some contact with Iran, Egypt, and North Africa, Americans generally knew and cared little about the area. The inevitable consequence was, on the one hand, an almost complete absence of interest and, on the other, a severe dearth of personnel fitted by training and experience to deal in a statesmanlike manner with Middle East questions as they might arise in the course of foreign relations. Inasmuch as the Middle East had occupied an important place in British foreign policy for at least a century and a half, there was much reluctance on the part of American officialdom, even after the close of World War II, to assume any direct responsibilities in this British sphere of interest.

Only as the decline of British imperial power and the importance to free world security of the Middle East came to be realized did the United States arrive at a more or less reluctant willingness to assume a measure of responsibility in the area. This was first manifested in relieving Britain of the burden of extending aid to hard-pressed Greece and Turkey. While this action proved to be of inestimable utility at a moment of crisis, it was clearly only a stopgap measure at a single crucial point in a contest that already had grown to global proportions. Free world security could on no reasonable grounds be regarded as having been attained by the setting up of the North Atlantic Treaty Organization for the defense of Europe or by assistance to Greece and Turkey. Security being indivisible, it would manifestly be of similar consequence to bring the Arab states, Iran, and Israel into a mutual defense system or at least to make sure of a preferential leaning toward the West in countries so strategically located.

For a task of this nature, as has been observed, the United States was poorly prepared. The measure of its unpreparedness is to be seen in the belief, prevalent but a few years ago and not by any means wholly dissipated today, that a spirit of mutual trust and interdependence could be induced, in countries so lacking as those of the Middle East in the elements of Western material culture, by means of the generous application of the Point Four concept. [See Reference Shelf Volume 23, Number 5, *The Point Four Program,* by W. M. Daniels—Ed.] In keeping with this idea, programs of technical and financial assistance were developed and in due course were put into effect on a contractual basis in most of the Middle East countries. It is not requisite here to undertake an appraisal of the Point Four scheme as a means of improving conditions of life in so-called underdeveloped countries. In some parts of the Middle East the program undoubtedly has conferred benefits of one kind or another. It is essential to note, however, that in view of many of the circumstances prevailing in the area at the period when Point Four was launched, it could not justifiably have been expected to produce the attitudes anticipated in what we may call the political sphere within the critical period of a few years. A brief review of the main factors which have exercised a circumscribing influence on efforts to bring all of the Middle East within the range of a free world security system will help to explain the lack of important progress thus far.

British Interests

In taking over certain of the responsibilities formerly regarded as lying within the British range of interest, the United States found itself heir to situations resulting from the long-time activities of Great Britain in the area. . . . At the same time, Great Britain was one of the founders of the North Atlantic Treaty Organization, and on this and other grounds was an indispensable partner in any scheme of defense of the free world. For these reasons, as well as for the sake of some measure of diplomatic collaboration from experienced hands, the United States, in establishing its own relations with Middle East governments, has been under the practical necessity of respecting the position still maintained by Britain in any part of the Middle East area. The inevitable consequence has been the transfer to the United States of a large portion of the suspicion and dislike that was attached to Great Britain as a "colonial" power by peoples still very conscious of their recent emancipation from British leading strings and hypersensitive, as are all young states, to any traces of influence of an imperialistic or restrictive nature. . . .

Whereas the problems arising from association with Great Britain were inherent in any direct approach by the United States to the states of the Middle East and could not have been avoided altogether, others, perhaps quite avoidable, have sprung from United States behavior with reference to certain other situations and developments within the area. The part played by the United States Government at the inception of the Zionist state of Israel, in the heart of the Arab world, is an instance particularly in point.

Israel

In Palestine, Jews, Arabs, and miscellaneous Christian elements had lived together in comparative amity for many centuries under the various regimes that successively were ascendant in the lands east of the Mediterranean. The rise of serious internal discord in this Holy Land, ironically enough, followed the first stages in political emancipation from the rule of the Ottoman Turks. Under British administration, after World War I, it was the fate of both Jews and Arabs in Palestine to find themselves segments of two much greater groups already politically conscious of their religious and ethnic inheritances and imbued with nationalistic urges. Zionism, on the one hand, and pan-Arabism, on the other, inspired disorders within Palestine which came to assume international dimensions. The events of World War II, which created the need for the resettlement of hundreds of thousands of European Jewish refugees and further contributed to the rise of independent Arab states in the Middle East, rendered it essential, no doubt, that Palestine should be partitioned in some fashion into Jewish and Arab segments. It was one of the great misfortunes of the contemporary world, however, that this could not have been accomplished by the British mandatory regime or by the United Nations in a peaceful and orderly manner. The instant recognition de facto by the President of the United States of the state of Israel proclaimed by Zionist leaders upon the voluntary termination of the British mandate on May 15, 1948, the defensive strength subsequently manifested by Israeli forces in the Arab war already in progress, and the annexation by Transjordan of the remainder of Arab Palestine brought an end to the issue of partition. At the same time these developments gave a large measure of fixity to one of the most bitter of all international feuds—kept alive by the plight of more than 800,000 homeless, stateless Arab refugees driven from their former homes in Palestine, and marked by frequent instances of border violence and by a close Arab boycott of everything pertaining to Israel.

In this extremely unfortunate situation the United States on its own account is deeply involved and committed. In an over-all sense, it is involved as the power most responsible for the security of the free world. But in the Arab-Israel controversy, which has a direct bearing on that security, it is committed as a partisan not only by sponsorship of Israel at the time of its inception but also by extensive financial support thereafter, without which the Zionist state could not possibly have continued to survive. Consequently, with respect to the building up in the Middle East of a security system related to that which now applies to the North Atlantic and Mediterranean areas, the United States is compelled to proceed under a major handicap.

Other Difficulties

The Israel-Arab imbroglio is by no means the only serious obstacle to the building up of a security system in the Middle East beyond the confines of Turkey. Numerous other influences have contributed to the growth of an unpromising situation in the area. These include attitudes toward the West engendered by the grafting of modern nationalist sentiment on the ancient trunk of Islam. They spring from memories of earlier forms of European exploitation. In some measure they result from envy of the advantages derived by Western countries from the utilization of Middle East oil resources. They stem, in part, from the countenance given by the United States and other members of the NATO group to France, for the sake of strategic air bases in North Africa, in its harsh efforts to restrain the nationalist aspirations of the Arabic populations in Tunis and Morocco. All of these and other difficulties less fundamental in character add up to the fact that most of the Middle East outside of Turkey cannot presently be counted upon to cooperate actively with the security system projected by the leading Atlantic Pact nations. Whether or in what way these handicaps can be overcome at all is a moot question. . . .

There is some evidence as time passes of an increasing measure of Anglo-American agreement on Middle East questions. As far as it goes, this is an excellent augury, for the Arab-Iranian states are not as yet definitely lost to the West. Temporizing cannot be continued indefinitely, however, without great risk of the dissipation of Western influence beyond recovery. Since neither Great Britain nor the United States is in a position to "go it alone," joint policy decisions of a consistent and enduring nature are called for and are not the less needed because they must take into account the diverse interests of other governments outside of the Middle East. . . .

The Present Task

Thus far, in undertaking to establish situations of strength in the Middle East, neither the United States nor Great Britain nor the two of them together with France, Greece, and Turkey and the African and Eastern Commonwealth nations have been prepared to move sufficiently from strength. Whatever may be the power potential of the United States and its NATO allies and associates in and beyond the Mediterranean, it cannot take the place of integrated, constructive, and consistent policy with respect to the Middle East. Even under the best of circumstances the allies will be hard put to maintain a substantial margin of favor and influence in the militarily "soft" yet strategically vital states of the area. The Middle East is so situated relative to the principal habitable parts of the world and bears such an important relationship to the balance of power among nations through its resources in petroleum that inevitably there will continue to be keen competition among rival power blocs for priority of influence in its . . . countries. In view of the fundamental needs and deficiencies of these countries, such competition almost certainly will continue to breed confusion and hesitation among the peoples of the area. Considering their long experience with the methods employed by great powers bent on consolidating their positions and advancing their national interests, there is little occasion for wonder that most of the states in this group, skeptical as to offers of friendship and protection and uncertain as to where the greater danger lies, prefer . . . to seek refuge in neutralism. In seeking to provide for its own security as well as that of the rest of the free world, the United States thus is confronted with a challenge of a major order.

GREAT POWER COMMITMENTS [2]

Within and outside the Middle East, the governments with a stake there have been reexamining and reappraising their military, economic, and political commitments. Two major lines of diplomatic action and maneuver have emerged; . . .

(1) Under United Nations auspices, efforts were set in motion to work out more effective measures for enforcement of the existing Arab-Israeli truce with the parties directly concerned. They were accompanied by cautious explorations to determine whether negotiations to remove basic obstacles to a permanent settlement could be put under way with any promise of success.

(2) Rival alliances in the area were buttressed or expanded by new accessions: the Baghdad Pact, linking four northern tier

[2] From "Middle East Commitments," by William T. Stone, editor, *Editorial Research Reports*. *Editorial Research Reports*. 1, no 18:335-43. May 9, 1956. Reprinted by permission.

nations [i.e. Iran, Pakistan, Iraq, and Turkey] with Great Britain, was reinforced by entry of the United States into the work of its permanent committees, although this country still refused to adhere to the treaty. The Cairo-led southern tier alliance linking Egypt with Syria and Saudi Arabia was expanded to include Yemen, the Arabian kingdom which flanks the British protectorate of Aden at the entrance to the Red Sea.

The big powers outside the region made a series of foreign policy statements that reflected conflicting interests and commitments on the one hand, and changing estimates of the situation in the Middle East on the other. Countries of the West narrowed the differences among themselves and strongly supported the UN peace moves, but their own divergent commitments made it difficult to agree on a common course of action. The Soviet Union hedged on—but did not withdraw—earlier Communist arms commitments to Egypt; faced with the danger of hostilities in Palestine, it offered to work toward a general arms embargo and to support UN efforts to find a peaceful settlement.

Communist Arms

The arms agreement under which Egypt has been obtaining military equipment from Czechoslovakia ended the monopoly of supply in the Middle East previously held by the Western powers. By opening a new and potentially large source of military equipment to the Arab states aligned with Egypt, the Soviet Union not only sought to undermine regional security arrangements of the Western powers, but also asserted its presence as a great power in the whole area stretching from the Eastern Mediterranean to the Persian Gulf. It was clear that Moscow intended henceforth to have a voice in decisions affecting that strategic sphere.

Moscow has been exerting the influence of a great power in the Mideast without either expanding or contracting its military commitments. The original commitments to Egypt have been carried out, and Soviet official spokesmen have continued to justify similar arrangements with other Arab states as commercial transactions. At the same time, the Soviet government seems to have avoided enlarging deliveries of military equipment to the area, and has been vague about future deliveries which would increase the imbalance created by the initial shipments. . . .

Obligations to Combat Aggression

Under the right of individual or collective self-defense, recognized in Article 51 of the UN Charter, the Western powers have assumed broad obligations to take concerted action, including the use of armed force, to resist aggression in specific areas of the Middle East and the Mediterranean. Three joint undertakings, in particular, embody direct military or political commitments.

Tripartite Declaration of 1950, whereby the United States, Great Britain, and France agreed to "take action both within and outside the United Nations" to prevent any violation of existing frontiers or armistice lines between Israel and the Arab states.

Protocol to the North Atlantic Treaty signed October 17, 1951, on the accession of Greece and Turkey, which extended the mutual security guarantees of the treaty to the territories of Turkey in the Near East and to the Mediterranean Sea.

Baghdad Pact, a regional security agreement signed February 24, 1955, by Turkey and Iraq, and subsequently adhered to by Great Britain, Pakistan, and Iran, which obligates the parties to "cooperate for their security and defense." The United States, not a formal member, has supported the aims of the pact and joined two of its working committees.

The three-power declaration of 1950 never had the effect of a binding treaty commitment. Framed as a joint statement of policy by the Western foreign ministers at a meeting in London on May 28, 1950, it laid down "fundamental principles" to guide the three governments in their dealings with Israel and the Arab states on questions of arms deliveries and frontier violations.

Reaffirming their opposition to an arms race, the Western powers declared they would control their deliveries of military equipment in such a way as to meet the legitimate needs of the countries of the Middle East for "internal security and self-defense" and permit them to play a part in the defense of the area as a whole. The 1950 declaration included the following specific pledge with respect to the frontiers between Israel and the Arab states:

The three governments . . . [declare] . . . their unalterable opposition to the use of force or threat of force by any of the states in that area. . . . Should they find that any of those states was preparing to violate frontiers or armistice lines, they would . . . immediately take action, both within and outside the United Nations, to prevent such violation.

With tension mounting in the Middle East, differences developed among the three Western powers as to the extent of the obligations they had assumed and as to means of preventing resort to force in the Arab-Israeli conflict. Great Britain urged the United States in March [1956] to make it clear that the Big Three would stand together in opposing any act of aggression in Palestine, by force if necessary.

Washington undertook to clarify its position in a White House statement, April 9, [1956] that placed primary emphasis on action through the United Nations.

The United States, in accordance with its responsibilities under the Charter of the United Nations, will observe its commitments within constitutional means to oppose any aggression in the area.

The United States is likewise determined to support and assist any nation which might be subjected to such aggression . . . [and] . . . is confident that other nations will act similarly in the cause of peace.

By emphasizing American responsibilities under the UN Charter, the White House clearly implied that any decision to take joint military action in the Middle East should be based on identification of the aggressor by the Security Council, which would require concurrence of all the permanent members, including the Soviet Union. The United States Government gave no indication of what action it might be prepared to take outside the United Nations, if a Soviet veto should prevent a decision by the Council.

By declaring that the United States would observe its commitments "within constitutional means," the White House statement suggested that President Eisenhower did not intend to send

American armed forces into action in the Middle East, independently or with the forces of other nations, without the approval of Congress.

British and U.S. Links to Baghdad Pact

The United States and Great Britain, while sharing a common interest in strengthening the security of the Middle East as a whole, have different commitments in the area. The American Government actively encouraged the development of a regional security arrangement among the northern tier states facing the Soviet Union, but did not itself become a party to the argreement. Britain, on the other hand, was the first country to adhere to the Baghdad Pact after it was promulgated by Turkey and Iraq in February 1955 and opened to accession by other countries,

The British Government had special reason to join the Baghdad defense group last year, as Iraq was pressing for termination of the Anglo-Iraqi alliance of 1930 two years in advance of its 1957 expiration date. Accordingly, at the time that Britain adhered to the Baghdad Pact, it signed a separate agreement with Iraq providing for immediate termination of the 1930 alliance, restoration of Iraqi sovereignty over British military and air bases in that country, and maintenance of "close cooperation" between the two governments.

The Baghdad Pact obligates its members to "cooperate for their security and defense," but the terms of the treaty embody no military commitments comparable to the mutual security guarantees of the North Atlantic alliance. Such defensive measures as the parties agree to take are to be the subject of special agreements among them. Last November the five member governments established a permanent organization, including a council, a secretariat, and special committees for joint military planning, economic cooperation, and anti-subversion activities.

The United States, while attempting to maintain its policy of "impartial friendship" in the Middle East, has drawn closer to the Baghdad Pact without accepting full membership. Washington was represented at the last meeting of the council, held in

Teheran . . . [in April 1956] by an observer group headed by Deputy Under Secretary of State Loy Henderson. During the meeting the United States accepted membership in the economic and anti-subversion committees, agreed to establish a military liaison group headed by a general or an admiral, and undertook to share in the administrative costs of the permanent organization.

Military Assistance and Special Commitments

The United States has been giving direct military assistance to the four northern tier countries now members of the Baghdad Pact. Separate mutual defense assistance agreements were concluded with Turkey, Iran, Iraq, and Pakistan between 1947 and 1954, and military shipments to those countries in fiscal 1955 were valued at $238 million. In addition, limited amounts of military equipment were made available until recently, under so-called "cash reimbursable agreements," to Israel and three Arab states—Egypt, Lebanon, and Saudi Arabia.

Under the cash agreements, purchases of arms may be made either through ordinary commercial channels or from the United States Government; each agreement specifies that the purchasing government will use the arms only for "purposes of internal security, and for self-defense"; all purchases, whether from private or governmental sources, are subject to export license controls. After the Egyptian arms deal with Czechoslovakia in September 1955, Israel submitted an urgent request to the United States for permission to purchase in this country substantial quantities of military equipment for "legitimate self-defense." However, export licenses to Israel were withheld under a general policy, laid down by President Eisenhower . . . [in] November [1955], of avoiding action that would "contribute to an arms competition in the Middle East, because such a race would not be in the interests of any of the participants." [This statement was issued at Denver, November 9, 1955—Ed.]

Certain other countries in the Middle East have been granted American export licenses this year for small shipments of arms previously ordered and paid for under cash reimbursable agreements. Eighteen light reconnaissance tanks were released for export to Saudi Arabia in February [1956]; State Department officials explained that the order, placed in April 1955, had been approved by the United States Government on August 25, and paid for on November 26. Failure of the United States to honor the commitment, according to Under Secretary Hoover, might have had an adverse effect on pending negotiations with Saudi Arabia for renewal of the American air base agreement with that country.

Other Western powers have continued to supply limited amounts of arms to countries of the Middle East within the terms of the 1950 declaration. France, with the approval of the United States, has made small shipments to Israel and currently is reported to be negotiating with that country for delivery of an undisclosed number of jet fighter planes. Great Britain has furnished technical aid and equipment to Iraq under its mutual assistance agreement, and has continued to subsidize the Arab Legion in Jordan.

Early this year the British Government sought to persuade King Hussein of Jordan to align that country with the Baghdad Pact nations. The British move was countered swiftly by Egypt, which attempted to bring Jordan into the Cairo-led alliance with Syria and Saudi Arabia. King Hussein, trying to maintain an independent position between the rival defense groups, turned down both proposals. However, on March 1 Hussein dismissed Sir John Bagot Glubb, the British officer who had developed the Arab Legion and served for thirty years as chief of staff of the Jordanian army. That unexpected move, apparently made under pressure from nationalist elements in the Arab Legion, not only impaired British prestige but also underscored the tenuous nature of political and military alignments in the Arab world.

A PACT FOR THE "NORTHERN TIER" [3]

The Premiers of Turkey, Iraq, Iran and Pakistan, and the British Foreign Secretary met . . . [in Baghdad during late November 1955] and drew a line across the Middle East's

[3] From "Baghdad Pact Completes Long Chain of Defenses," by Kennett Love, New York *Times* correspondent. New York *Times*. p E5. November 27, 1955. Reprinted by permission.

northern tier against a southward march of Russian Communist influence.

The delegates were acutely aware that the line, mapped more than two years [previously] by the United States, was not enough to keep the Soviet Union from leapfrogging into the Arab hinterland with arms sales and offers of economic aid.

At an organizational conference of the Council of the Baghdad Pact . . . the representatives of the five member nations drafted a blueprint for a wall to be built on the line—a political, military and economic organization with permanent deputies and a secretariat . . . in Baghdad.

Before returning home delegates let it be known that United States membership and aid would be required to build the planned organization into an effective reality and that the adherence of other Arab nations besides Iraq would be necessary to give it a firm regional foundation.

The communiqué announcing the creation of the pact organization was perhaps deliberately vague. In contrast, the "not-for-attribution" statements by spokesmen for the member and observer delegations on the need for United States and Arab adherence were deliberately pointed and explicit.

The pact is part of a chain of United States-sponsored defense treaty organizations reaching along the Soviet bloc's land perimeter from Norway to the Philippines. It is linked through Turkey with the North Atlantic Treaty Organization, of which the United States is a member, and through Pakistan with the Southeast Asia defense pact, of which the United States is also a member.

The United States supplies military and economic aid to the Baghdad Pact members under prior bilateral agreements. The pact was proposed by Secretary of State Dulles after his Middle Eastern tour in the spring of 1953. Turkey signed an alliance with Pakistan in April 1954, but it was superseded by the present pact, which began with an alliance between Turkey and Iraq signed . . . [on February 24, 1955].

The pact, renewable after five years for further five-year terms, did not provide for a joint command over the armies along its 3,000-mile front. The still undetailed outlines of its structure are based on a permanent policy-making council at the ministerial level whose members are to be represented at the headquarters here by deputies of ambassadorial rank.

The ministerial council is to have a military and an economic committee and a secretariat. The United States has promised continued support and holds out the possibility of eventual membership.

One of the American formulators of the pact has conceded that it was conceived more as a political and ideological *cordon sanitaire* against Soviet encroachment than as a military front against possible armed aggression. The Baghdad Pact is not expected in the foreseeable future to be able to hold or even significantly to delay a Soviet attack, but the commitment of its members to the Western Allies is regarded as a barrier against subversion.

The desire of the Middle Eastern member governments for United States aid in combatting subversion and suppressing internal unrest was a major motive for joining the pact, perhaps the primary motive in the case of Iran.

The strongest member of the pact is Britain. . . . Of the regional members, the Turks have the strongest army, believed to number near its World War II strength of 850,000 troops.

Pakistan has an army of 190,000; Iran 125,000, and Iraq somewhat more than 40,000. The Iranian Army is the weakest link, having recently undergone a sweeping purge of subversives in its officer cadres, unfortunately losing many of its ablest and therefore most dangerous young men to prisons and firing squads.

Although the four Middle Eastern members of the pact have different languages and traditions, they are united by the Moslem religion and a common sympathy with the desire of the United States and Britain to keep Soviet influence from supplanting their own.

The pact's effectiveness depends primarily on the United States, and its strength is thus potential and not actual. If the United States remains aloof too long, the pact will disintegrate and the ensuing disillusionment will give a severe setback to both United States and British prestige in the area.

As it stands, the pact has caused a split in the Arab world. Egypt, feeling abandoned by the West in favor of Iraq, her arch-rival for Arab leadership, has bitterly opposed the pact and has veered toward neutralism in the "cold war." Syria, Saudi Arabia and Yemen have sided with Egypt, while Jordan and Lebanon have thus far eschewed taking sides in the Arab rift.

Why has the United States risked leaving the Baghdad Pact in a state of suspended animation despite the fact that its creation has made the Arab hinterland vulnerable to Communist penetration?

Ambassador Waldemar J. Gallman, United States observer at the pact conference, told the member delegations his govern-ment believed it could contribute more by remaining outside. United States spokesmen gave two reasons for this belief:

(1) United States adherence might further estrange Egypt and her Arab allies.

(2) A United States alliance with Iraq, the only Arab League member of the pact, would evoke an Israeli counter-demand for a mutual defense treaty, which could become an issue in . . . [the 1956] presidential elections. A treaty with Israel under the present conditions would cause the Arabs, including Iraq, to reject alliances with the United States and make them increasingly receptive to Soviet overtures.

This reasoning led the Baghdad delegates, including Iraq, to the conclusion that settlement of the Palestine problem was the third major requirement of a viable pact—after United States and Arab adherence to the treaty.

THE UNITED STATES TAKES OVER [4]

In the Middle East it has long been said that "the British act; the Americans take the blame." The British have been the power on the spot. British forces were in Suez, the Sudan, Palestine, Jordan, Iraq, the Persian Gulf, Cyprus—a formidable network.

[4] From "U.S. and Britain at Odds on the Middle East," by Dana Adams Schmidt, New York *Times* Washington correspondent. New York *Times*. p E5. April 1, 1956. Reprinted by permission.

British economic interests have been paramount. And the Americans, without much argument, have accepted the role of junior partners and have followed the British lead.

Now it appears that the United States is rapidly tiring of its junior partner role. British leadership has led steadily from disaster to disaster to the point where the network of British forces in the Middle East is no longer formidable. The British are out of Suez [last troops left in June 1956—Ed.], out of the Sudan, out of Palestine. They still have airbase rights in Jordan and access to bases in Iraq, and wield a good deal of influence in both countries; but their position has grown steadily weaker.

In the Persian Gulf there have been anti-British riots in Bahrein and conflict with Saudi Arabia over the Buraimi Oasis; the immense British economic stake in the Persian Gulf is threatened. In Cyprus a bomb is found in the British governor's bed and British forces are regularly pelted with stones and more lethal objects.

Now the Russians are attempting to penetrate the positions of influence vacated by the British. The United States is being forced, in defense of its own and general Western interests, to assume the role of senior partner in the Middle East.

The United States' approach differs from Britain's because the sources of its strength and weaknesses are different.

At the risk of oversimplification one may say that British policy in the Middle East (like French policy in North Africa) derives from the need to defend Britain's remaining special privileges and positions. The United States does not have such privileges and positions.

This fact is supplemented by the United States' military aid program for Turkey, to whom it has supplied more military equipment and related aid since 1947 than Britain has delivered to the indigenous armies of all the countries of the Middle East since World War I. Also the United States has begun in a small way to displace Britain as Iraq's source of military supplies.

Perhaps more important when it comes to wielding influence, the United States' economic position as extractor of oil (about equal to Britain's in importance) is supplemented increasingly by its role as purveyor of economic aid.

Most basically, the United States, unlike Britain, does not carry the burden of past and present efforts to suppress or limit the sovereignty of the people of the area. On the contrary, the United States used its influence to persuade the French during World War II to grant full sovereignty to Lebanon and Syria and more recently to persuade the British to leave Suez.

On the other hand, the United States seems to have inherited most of the conflict of motives and interests that plagued the British from the time they subscribed to the Balfour Doctrine acknowledging Palestine as a Jewish national home to the time they gave up their mandate in Palestine. Today the British are out of Palestine. Until recently they have found it tempting to identify themselves fully with the Arabs. The United States stands committed to the preservation of Israel.

Against this background the United States has recently been trying to take the initiative in Palestine through diplomatic channels. By quiet talks with Israeli and Arab leaders the State Department has tried to put across the Johnston plan for joint Arab and Israeli development of the Jordan River Valley, and, more generally, to persuade Israelis and Arabs that the time has come to start settling their differences.

This has not worked, partly because Americans, British and French have not been pulling together. [Recently] the differences between the United States and British approaches have been highlighted by British efforts to put a stop to retreats, to show that they can still be firm.

Thus, the British deported Archbishop Makarios from Cyprus —and Washington reacted by expressing sympathy for the feelings of the Greek people and by urging the British to continue negotiating.

Britain let it be known she had completed plans for military intervention to put a prompt end to any Israeli-Arab war, but Washington, preoccupied by its own approach to the problem, dissociated itself from any such plans. Finally a spokesman of the British Foreign Office uttered some plain hard words about Premier Gamal Abdel Nasser of Egypt.

Washington officials acknowledged sadly in this case that the British were probably right. Up to quite recently Washington has clung to the idea that Premier Nasser was fundamentally peace-loving and oriented to the West, and that if peace between Israel and the Arab states was ever to be achieved it would be through Premier Nasser's enlightened leadership. But it has become progressively disenchanted by the Premier's technique of talking peace and pro-Westernism in private contacts with Westerners, and then acting and speaking in public against the interests of the West, against peace with Israel, and for neutralism. But the American officials observed that it was a mistake for the British to say all this out loud just now.

This is only an introduction to the points of friction between Britain and the United States in the Middle East.

One of the most significant of these is the question whether arms should be supplied to Israel to offset the arms Egypt is getting from Communist Czechoslovakia. The British—and also the French—feel the United States has been less than frank in delaying its answers to Israel's request while asserting that it has no objection if the "traditional suppliers" of arms to the Middle East send arms to Israel. The British and French feel the United States is in this way trying to shift to them the blame—in Arab eyes—for arming the Israelis. . . .

The United States Government was irritated by the British Government's recent attempts to roar like a nineteenth-century lion, particularly because it was busy trying, not too successfully, to launch a new approach to the Palestine problem through the United Nations. This was an overt follow-up to earlier attempts through diplomatic channels to make American leadership felt in the Middle East.

While formally supporting the American move, the British and French privately look down their noses sourly at the idea of "another United Nations commission." . . .

The diplomats like to stress that what the Americans and British have in common in the Middle East is far more important than the differences between them, that they are, after all united in their objectives even if not in their methods. But the outlook is not encouraging.

BRITISH PROBLEMS [5]

[In early January 1956] Britain's new Foreign Secretary, Selwyn Lloyd, called eight of his top ambassadors back from the Middle East for a long, hard look at Britain's halting policy toward that region.

[Soon Lloyd would] sail with Prime Minister Eden to the United States for top-level talks with President Eisenhower, Secretary of State Dulles and other American leaders. There the chief architects of Western foreign policy would try, jointly, to breathe some life into their Middle Eastern ideas, . . . widely criticized as moribund if not deceased. . . .

The Middle East today is Britain's number one "headache" area and it was an inauspicious time for Mr. Lloyd to assume his stewardship—even with Sir Anthony, a life-long Middle East expert, closely watching developments across the narrow width of Downing Street.

How to devise new "tactics" or even a new "strategy" was the problem. Mr. Lloyd, fresh from his last post as Minister of Defense, ordered strict secrecy about his meeting, while Prime Minister Eden seemed determined not to let the Labor Opposition "smoke out" his new ideas in debate prior to his visit to General Eisenhower at the end of the month.

The chief criticisms of Britain's Middle East policy center on these points:

(1) Britain depends too much on the backing of aging and reactionary Arab politicians whose days of power in their countries are numbered.

(2) Britain has either not offered or not provided enough economic-technical aid to its "friends" in the Middle East."

(3) Britain still hews too closely to the favorite Dulles panacea for foreign relations, "pactomania," such as the shaky Baghdad Pact, which is the keystone to British policy in the area.

[5] From "Britain Seeks Way out of Middle East Crisis," by Benjamin Welles, New York *Times* correspondent. New York *Times.* p E5. January 8, 1956. Reprinted by permission.

(4) Britain's political intelligence service in the area is either woefully weak compared with the past or else it is ignored by the Whitehall statesmen.

British diplomats admit to some if not all of these charges, but they insist that British Middle East policy is still logical and wise.

The Foreign Office, for instance, concentrates on the eight-year-old "cold war" between Israel and her Arab neighbors. Officials point out that Sir Anthony offered in recent speech to mediate between the two antagonists if they would "compromise" their struggle.

The longer the profitless Arab-Israeli clash goes on, say the British, the longer all other Middle East problems will fester. "Resolve the Arab-Israeli war first and you will see all the other pieces falling into place," they declare.

Officially, the Foreign Office does not agree that Britain is trying to "court" the Arabs. Privately, officials will admit that British power, prestige and hopes in the Middle East center far more on the Arab peoples than on Israel.

British statesmen, traditionally "realistic," point out that the 40 million Arabs in the Middle East not only own and control the oil that Europe so desperately needs, but also control a powerful bloc of votes in the United Nations. Israel, with a population of 2 million and very little oil, by contrast controls a single vote in the United Nations.

Meanwhile, the British have hung their diplomatic clothes on the hickory limb of the Baghdad Pact: A five-nation anti-Communist alliance embracing Britain, Turkey, Iraq, Iran and Pakistan. . . .

Britain, confronted with mounting anti-Western feeling throughout the area where once her word was law, has joined the club and is seeking from the "inside" to consolidate her position, influence and economic plans.

To do this, though, British statesmen know that the Baghdad Pact must be transformed from a weak military alliance into a flourishing community of prospering, stable nations that are "pro-Western" because their masses perceive the benefits of such a policy and not because a few leaders have imposed it on them.

However, Britain alone does not have the resources needed to spark the Baghdad group into life.

The main aim of British policy in the Middle East therefore will undoubtedly be to close the Arab-Israeli gap by diplomatic pressure, with the prospect of broad-scale economic help via the Baghdad Pact to be held out as the reward.

British diplomats say that more leading men in the Arab capitals and in Israel now want a settlement than at any time in the last eight years.

In British eyes the key to this basic problem is how to persuade Premier Gamal Abdel Nasser of Egypt to accept United States-British mediation. If he could accept it, they hint, Britain would urge Nuri as-Said, the Iraq Premier, and other Arab leaders not to "jump" Colonel Nasser by accusing him of "betraying" the Arab cause.

In turn, they suggest, the United States would have to influence David Ben-Gurion, the leader of Israel, to adopt a more moderate, compromising attitude if Israel is to win the peace he says she wants.

THE SOVIET'S ENTRANCE [6]

In the framework of Soviet foreign relations, the countries of the Near and Middle East fall into two groups: Russia's contiguous neighbors, and the others. This distinction between direct neighbors and more distant lands has been decisive in Soviet postwar policy. . . .

Roughly half of the 90 million population of the Near and Middle East live in the countries [which are] Russia's neighbors. The other half comprise the Arab nations and Israel, the latter with a population of close to 2 million.

[6] From "Soviet Policy in the Middle East," by David J. Dallin, author of numerous books on Soviet Russia. *Middle Eastern Affairs.* 4:337-44. November 1955. Reprinted by permission.

In marked contrast to its attitude toward its neighbor countries, Moscow does not view the nations of this second group as potential satellites, and will not consider them so as long as the present world situation remains unchanged and no great new conflict breaks out. Membership in the Soviet family of nations is not being planned at present for any of the Near and Middle Eastern nations of this second group; they are not faced with a choice of being satellites or free nations.

The dilemma facing these countries is rather one of partisanship with the Western bloc, or neutrality. The supreme goal of Soviet policy in this part of the world is to detach one small nation after another from any alliance with Britain and the United States. Moscow will not be satisfied until the anti-Western neutralism which now prevails in South Asia is embraced by the independent Near and Middle East. In this area the Soviet methods of influencing governments and peoples are more subtle, friendly, and helpful, and the reaction to the Soviet *démarches* is therefore more conciliatory. The nations of this area do not feel directly menaced by aggression on the part of the Soviet Union; they have a free choice. Communism, although alive in both the Arab and the Israeli worlds, is too weak to be a threat; in these areas Moscow fosters movements of a national type in which the "evils of capitalism" are overshadowed by "anti-imperialist," anti-American, and anti-British slogans.

The underlying issue affecting the Soviet attitude toward developments in the Near and Middle East is that of East or West. The problem of the abject poverty of the masses of the population, the political system, "feudalism" and "capitalism" have been relegated to the background; paramount are the issues affecting postwar international tensions. In its search for anti-Western support the Soviet Government is prepared to ally itself with any anti-democratic monarchy and any dictatorial, even racist, regime, and to approve any bellicose trend, if such action would help to detach one or another nation from a pro-Western orientation.

When the Arab League emerged after the war, it was violently attacked in the Soviet press as a "stronghold of reaction" and a tool of British policy. In the contest between the Arabs and

Israel in 1947-1948, the Soviet Government favored the partition of Palestine and the creation of an independent Jewish state because this would weaken Britain. Later this gesture was used as proof of the farsightedness and progressivism of Leninism-Stalinism on national issues. As time passed, however, a careful balancing of the Arab and Israeli sides became more and more difficult.

Soviet envoys in the Arab countries were ordered to avoid friction with the Moslems, to make regular visits to mosques, and to stress the affinity between certain religious groups of the Soviet Union and those of Asia and Africa. The Orthodox clergy, too, assisted in the grand-scale Soviet drive to win footholds in the Middle East. The old Russian Palestine Society, founded about a hundred years ago, and which had accumulated considerable property in Palestine, was revived in 1952 under the name of the Palestine Archeological Society. Its ecclesiastical envoys soon came to Jerusalem to claim the rights and privileges it had had in the pre-revolutionary era. Large sums were expended for repair of church property in both Israel and Jordan; quantities of religious books were distributed; aged monks and nuns were taken under care. The Soviet envoy in Israel and his staff attended church services regularly. At the same time Russian priests visited Nazareth and established contact with Armenian and Syrian "sister-churches." In July 1950 the Lebanese Government recognized the legality of Soviet claims to old Russian property in Lebanon.

The Soviet position vis-à-vis the state of Israel, essentially a matter of foreign policy, is interwoven with an internal issue, namely, the regime's attitude toward Jews and Zionism in Russia. As the tensions of the cold war mounted and antagonism toward the West began to overshadow all other problems in Moscow, Stalin's government saw the Jewish population in Russia as the bearers of pro-Western trends and Western ideas, and even as partisans of the Western type of democracy. How closely international affairs were tied up with internal policies became obvious when a large Jewish crowd in Moscow, in defiance of the government, staged an enthusiastic demonstration in honor of Golda Meyerson, the first Israeli envoy to Moscow.

While never expressing his real attitude toward Israel in so many words, in 1948 Stalin began to increase his anti-Jewish drive at home and abroad, merging his personal dislikes with the world-wide objectives of a movement of which he was the leader. As persecution of the Jews mounted in Russia, all pro-Israeli trends and activities in the Soviet Union as well as in the satellites were violently suppressed. In February 1953, three weeks before his death, Stalin broke off diplomatic relations with Israel, using as a pretext the bombing of the building which housed the Soviet mission in Tel Aviv.

Since Stalin's death Soviet policy toward the Arab nations and Israel has changed but slightly. In the first months of confusion, diplomatic relations with Israel were resumed (July 1953) and the fight against Zionism in the satellites was abated. The period of weakness and the attempts at concilation, usually associated with the name of Georgi Malenkov, did not, however, last long. When Malenkov's star faded (since mid-1954) and Khrushchev took over leadership, new vigor was instilled into Soviet foreign policy. "Priority for heavy industry" —the formula under which Malenkov was dismissed and Bulganin became premier—actually meant the inauguration of a foreign policy which, while it avoided direct military entanglements, initiated competition with the West in the task of industrializing and arming backward countries. There has been grand-scale investment of Soviet capital in China; metallurgical plants are being built by Soviet engineers in India; industrial help is being offered the Arab nations.

At the same time export of arms to anti-Western governments is being fostered. Moscow itself has refrained from trade in arms, preferring to use the satellites for this delicate job in order to avoid unnecessary trouble. Among the satellites only two, East Germany and Czechoslovakia, are able to produce and export modern arms. Since German arms would be highly unpopular abroad at this time, the war industry of Czechoslovakia (the expanded Skoda works) serves as the Soviet arm in the munitions trade.

The Bandung conference of twenty-nine Asian and African nations which took place in April 1954, about two months

after Malenkov's dismissal, accentuated the anti-Western drive.
On April 16, 1955 the Soviet government published its statement on "security in the Near and Middle East" which, while
it contained no new ideas and outlined no new political positions, marked the start of a new large-scale diplomatic and
political offensive.

The Soviet offensive now centers around Egypt, the leading
Arab nation. Britain has erroneously assumed that accession to
Egyptian demands and withdrawal of British forces from the
Suez Canal would pacify the Arab world and reduce the fever of
nationalism that has taken hold of the Egyptian intelligentsia in
the last few years. The British-Egyptian agreement signed in
1954 provided for the evacuation of British forces in the com-
paratively short period of twenty months, so that after a long
era of British troops on Egyptian soil this Arab nation would
have regained complete independence. The Soviet Government
made abundant use of the mounting nationalist feelings in Egypt
and proved to be more right than London. Egypt did not, after
the conclusion of the agreement with Britain, abandon its anti-
Western position; indeed, it moved closer to the Soviet Union.

Working behind the scenes, the Soviet envoys in the Middle
East accomplished a coup in the summer of 1955 in piloting a
cooperation of three Arab nations—Egypt, Syria and Saudi
Arabia. Against internal and external objections, in particular
on the part of Iraq, Egypt and Syria signed a "defense pact" on
November 7, 1955. The material basis of the pact was the
supplying of arms by Czechoslovakia to the two Arab nations,
on financial terms agreed upon with the help of Soviet diplomatic representatives.

In its effort to lure Egypt from the West and demonstrate
the advantages of collaboration with Moscow, the Soviet Government, in the summer of 1955, arranged for wide-scale trade
operations in favor of the Cairo regime. Communist China
bought Egyptian cotton in the amount of 8 million Egyptian
pounds ($23 million). In a similar operation, Czechoslovakia
traded Czech arms for Egyptian cotton and rice. It is doubtful
whether, from an economic point of view, these trade operations,

which involve long-term credits, represent anything but substantial losses to the Communist nations. The transactions were a purely political affair the expense of which will be written off in the same manner as the cost of armies, navies, and air forces.

When the Egyptian-Czechoslovak arms deal became known and the world press attacked Moscow for its dangerous venture in the Middle East, official Soviet publications reacted in a characteristic way. Defending Czechoslovakia and Egypt, and stressing the latter's "sovereign right" to buy whatever arms it wants wherever it wants to, the Soviet press never so much as mentioned against whom the Arab nations were arming and what kind of a war was in the making if supplying of arms to Egypt in great quantities should continue for a considerable time. While pretending to "fight for peace" everywhere, including the Middle East, the Soviet press did not mention Israel as the target of the Soviet arms supplies. If a war should break out in this part of the world the sympathies of the Soviet regime, although never stated explicitly, will be on the Egyptian-Syrian side; in so far as assistance can be given without risk of outright involvement in war, the two Arab nations, rather than Israel, will enjoy Soviet help.

It would be an exaggeration to say that by its spectacular *démarches* of the last few months Moscow has been intentionally staging a world war. On the other hand, Moscow would not be unhappy to see the outbreak of a war between local forces in which superiority would lie with the anti-Western bloc. And when the day arrives for settling the conflict, the Soviet Government would expect to be invited to participate and have a voice in the settlement negotiations, as she had in the case of the settlement of the Korean and Indo-Chinese wars.

A few years ago Vyacheslav Molotov stated that there was no international issue or territory in which the Soviet Union was not interested. For a long time Soviet Russia has been excluded from the Mediterranean and the Middle East. Its aim now is to obtain a place in the African sun and secure a foothold there which it can widen in the future.

A NEW STRUGGLE SHAPES UP [7]

Russia's lethal giveaway program in the Middle East, with its disastrous effort on Western hegemony there and its implicit threat of war, is of American design and manufacture.

The design stolen by the Russians and malevolently embellished by them was the successful American appeal to the vanity of the Arabs by the offer, accepted by Iraq in the spring of 1954, to supply arms without political strings. This shallow maneuver succeeded, as intended, in inducing Iraq to participate in a mutual-assistance treaty with Turkey and Pakistan [the Baghdad Pact] allied to NATO. Participation of any Arab state in an Allied Middle East defense agreement had until then been strenuously opposed by Egypt and other members of the Arab League. As important as the assurance of United States arms to Iraq was Iraq's displacement of Egypt as the center of the Arab world and of Allied wooing. The agreement split the Arab League—a split which the United States hoped ultimately would lead to Arab adherence, one by one, to a military alliance with Turkey and the West. The anticipated benefits have not materialized. Instead of sealing off the Soviet Union, against whom the pact was directed, the agreement opened the doors of the Middle East barred to Russia since time immemorial.

Today, in every Arab country, where communism is prohibited and punishable by imprisonment or death, the Arab governments themselves have become the principal admirers and defenders of the Soviet Union. How was the anomaly produced?

The catalyst was the so-called "northern tier" defense pact, based on Turkey and Pakistan, since joined by Iraq, Britain, and Iran. Instead of containing the Soviet Union, it pushed the "neutralism" of Asia and the Arab bloc, hitherto passive, into an "activism" of which the . . . Czechoslovak-Egyptian arms deal is only one startling result.

Egypt was not the only country caught unaware and wounded in its national pride by the United States-Iraq arms deal and

[7] From "War in the Middle East," Part I: "Russia's Lethal Giveaway," by Lillie Shultz, director of Nation Associates and correspondent on the Middle East. *Nation.* 181:431-5. November 19, 1955. Reprinted by permission.

the subsequent Middle East pact. The inclusion of Pakistan, foe of India, as a keystone in the arrangement profoundly offended the sensibilities of Nehru. This common resentment in 1954 forged the loose *ad hoc* relationship between India and Egypt into a hard bloc against the United States. The leader of the great democratic experiment in India, whose strongest claim to world imagination has been his morality, became the sponsor and ally of Nasser, head of Egypt's military dictatorship.

Seeking a way to express independence of the West, to promote peace and to improve Asian-Arab conditions, Nehru conceived the Bandung conference, held in the spring of 1955 with the participation of sixteen countries, including Communist China. It was at Bandung that India sold morality short when it refused to invite Israel under the threat of Arab withdrawal. It was at Bandung that India permitted passage, without a dissenting vote, of an Arab resolution condemning Israel. It was at Bandung that Nasser, cosseted by Nehru, met Chou En-lai and received his first V. I. P. treatment from top Communist officialdom.

The turning point was Bandung, which produced the shower of invitations to Nasser by Russia and its satellites leading to the consummation of the Czech arms deal with Egypt. But Bandung was by no means the starting point. Russia has always coveted a warm-water port and a role in the Middle East. Since the end of World War II, it has served repeated notice to the West of its intention to push Britain out of the Middle East and itself to fill the vacuum. Russian support of Palestine partition in 1947 was part of this over-all purpose. The Jews seeking a state were breaking Britain's hold on the Middle East. So Russia supported them. As upsurging Arab nationalism created further pressure on Britain's entrenched position, Russian support shifted to the Arab side—a shift made easier by Israel's abandonment of its neutralist policy in favor of identification with the West.

Since 1950 Russia's tactics in the UN on successive occasions "saved" the Arab states from resolutions requiring direct negotiation with Israel on peace in general or on settlement of specific conflicts. Each such "victory" has been widely publicized in the Arab press and appropriate thanks given to the Russians.

In 1952 the Russians made a bold bid to establish consanguinity with the Arabs by launching their domestic campaign against the Jews. It was not, however, until the United States set the example in Iraq that the Russians found the key which unlocked the door to the Middle East—the appeal to vanity through arms. . . .

Egypt claims it accepted the Czechoslovak offer only after it failed . . . [in June 1955] to obtain $27 million worth of weapons from the United States. . . .

Not to be overlooked are the terms of the arrangement. The weapons are priced at one fifth to one tenth of what they would cost in the West. The arms deal is primarily a barter arrangement—Egyptian cotton and rice for arms—sealed by a small cash payment of one million pounds sterling. It is this barter aspect which is making a strong appeal to other countries, Middle Eastern and Asian, who have no hard currency and to whom the Communists have now made similar offers. . . .

Economic Aid

The arms offers have been buttressed by proffers of economic aid, based largely on barter or on low-rate long-term loans. Russia has offered Egypt help in building the high dam at Aswan on a barter deal plus a 3 per cent long-term loan, as against a more exigent financial arrangement offered by the International Bank for Reconstruction and Development, which estimates the cost at between $1.25 billion and $1.5 billion. Syria is being lured by Russian offers to purchase its surplus products on long-term loans. . . .

For the first time in history a Soviet legation will be posted in Yemen. Negotiations to this end are now going forward. . . .

Soviet economic penetration of Egypt has already begun and does not await the scheduled visit of Nasser to Russia in the spring. Cairo has concluded a series of barter arrangements with the Soviet bloc for the exchange of Egyptian cotton for Russian petroleum products, Hungarian locomotive and consumer goods, Polish coal, East German construction equipment and consumer goods.

Under a three-year arrangement with China, Egypt will sell $30 million worth of cotton and will buy only $6 million worth of Chinese products. China will pay cash in pound sterling for $24 million worth of Egyptian cotton.

Good-will missions are carrying the Soviet message forward in all the Arab countries.

None of the Russian offers is made conditional on military or political alliances. It is the lack of such formal conditions, the reverse of the American tactic, which is allaying the principal Arab fear—that of foreign domination. In the space of two months, the Russians have reversed the course of centuries in the most formidable direct challenge to Western holdings and power in the area.

As a result the effectiveness of the "northern tier" defense pact is lessened, if not destroyed; French Morocco is subject to an incursion of Soviet arms via Egypt, the principal supporter of the Moroccan nationalists; the Suez Canal zone is threatened with immobilization; the outbreak of an Arab-Israel war is possible which may involve the West.

How to resolve these problems and how to stop the further Russian penetration of a continent rich in oil, minerals, strategic communications, and ripe for Communist persuasion by reason of the appalling social and economic conditions of life in all the Arab countries—that is the dilemma of the West. . . .

The American Dilemma

The resulting overwhelming American dilemma is largely of our own making, deriving from a policy of deliberate blindness to the revolution against colonialism in Asia, Africa, and the Middle East, and to the wishes and needs of its peoples. To the securing of military bases every consideration . . . involved in true security had been subordinated.

The Russians have now demonstrated that they cannot be contained by Allied military pacts, and the Arab governments have demonstrated, as one observer wittily put it, that they cannot be bought but only rented to the highest bidder.

This situation we ourselves helped to create by shoring up unstable and unworthy governments through a policy of appeasement which began with the Palestine question in 1947. The United States vote for partition was a reluctant one, put through by President Truman against the machinations of his own State Department, which was concerned lest American oil rights in Saudi Arabia be jeopardized and which was also being prodded by the British. Since that time the State Department diehards have tried to live down that vote by repeatedly yielding to Arab intransigence. It is true that the United States has been generous in its economic support of Israel. That support can be attributed less to the State Department than to the broader understanding shown by Congress.

Although obviously preferring an Arab-Israel peace, yet not wishing to offend the Arabs, the State Department has never made any real attempt to consummate peace. On more than one occasion it has been an undercover ally of the Arabs in preventing the passage of UN resolutions which would have brought the issue to a head. Although the United States is the source of the principal funds that have kept alive the Arab refugees, and although it has acknowledged that these refugees cannot go back to Israel and would not be happy there, it has made only desultory attempts to seek a permanent solution and has permitted the Arab governments to continue to use the refugee issue as a political football for eight successive years, while refugee demoralization grew apace and with it Communist penetration. . . .

What hope there exists of stopping the Russians effectively is through the immediate settlement of the Palestine war; the abandonment, for the moment at least, of the American obsession with military pacts as the first step in the road to security; and the concentration on large-scale development for the area.

The settlement of the Palestine war would have the effect of ending the intense rivalry among the Arab states for allegedly "defensive" weapons against Israel on which the Russians have played so successfully.

Precisely because this is a moment of intense crisis, the UN should be brought into special session for the sole purpose of bringing about direct Arab-Israel peace talks. This is the primary function of the UN which has not dealt seriously with the threat to Middle-East peace since the armistice agreements of 1949—primarily because neither Britain nor the United States wished to offend the Arabs.

The Arab states will, of course, resist the effort but Arab intransigence can no longer be allowed to be decisive. Today it is the Western alliance which needs peace, even more profoundly than Israel. Nor can any member of the UN afford to oppose a serious effort to produce peace negotiations. This includes the Soviet Union. Here is as good an issue as any with which to test the Soviet "new look." At the same time the challenge should [be] put to India, principal advocate of peace within the UN, to rally Asia behind such a move. . . .

In exchange for peace the United States should be prepared to offer through the UN: (1) large-scale technical assistance, with no strings attached, to Egypt and the whole area; (2) a large reconstruction and development fund for underdeveloped territories; (3) the assurance of the revision of American economic policy, taking into account the needs of the underdeveloped territories and their inability to pay in dollars. Encompassed within the concept of a peace settlement must be the *a priori* assurance of the permanent rehabilitation in Arab lands of the Arab refugees, compensated for their lost possessions in Israel.

And if the Arabs refuse, what then? The Arabs cannot afford to be isolated and made the de facto satellites of the Soviet bloc. The United States could insure that isolation by utilizing both its influence with the members of the UN and the machinery provided in the Charter to prevent a threat to the peace. It could also refuse to continue to support 900,000 Arab refugees through a program which successive reports of the

United Nations Works and Relief Agency have indicated is inadequate and demoralizing unless the refugees are permanently resettled. . . .

THE PROBLEM OF THE SUEZ CANAL [8]

The 106 miles of tepid water and hot sand between Port Said and Suez in Egypt became again . . . [at the end of July 1956] the focus of national rivalries and personal ambitions.

President Gamal Abdel Nasser of Egypt seized control of a supposedly neutralized international waterway—the Suez Canal —and announced nationalization of the Suez Canal Company, which has operated the canal throughout the eighty-seven years since it was built. The implications of this move were obviously world-wide and portended a major crisis in the Middle East.

The strip of man-made ditch between Port Said on the Mediterranean and Suez at the head of the Red Sea is a sea level canal with Egyptian territory on both sides. . . .

Because of its sinuous curves, its great length and narrow width, the canal can be easily blocked—as it has been in the past—by beached or wrecked ships, by mines or by mud banks or silting, or by the sand storms of the desert.

Ships use great care and are piloted carefully, by more than one hundred polylingual pilots. . . .

The vast British airfields and supply and operational bases, recently evacuated by British uniformed personnel but still manned by some British civilian employees, were concentrated chiefly in a seventy-by-fifty-mile area. . . . [Many] points astride the Canal were sites of British power, now under Egyptian control.

The economic importance of Suez is that it provides a short cut from Atlantic and Mediterranean to the Indian and Pacific oceans. The distance from New York to Red Sea points is reduced 6,700 miles by use of the Suez Canal. Tankers bound from New York to Persian Gulf oil fields save approximately

[8] From "Suez Vital Link in World Trade," by Hanson W. Baldwin, New York *Times* military correspondent. New York *Times*. p E5. July 29, 1956. Reprinted by permission.

3,500 miles each way. Translated into terms of costs, this means that a laden Liberty ship bound from Boston to Karachi—according to the Suez Canal Company—would pay $5,400 in canal tolls but would save some fourteen days time, which would cost approximately $28,000.

The Suez Canal has increased in economic importance since World War II, in part because of the development of Middle Eastern oil fields. Prior to World War II the Panama Canal and the Suez Canal carried about the same amount of traffic; today Suez carries three times as much traffic as Panama, and its toll charges of less than one cent a ton-mile for laden ships are about half Panama's charges. In 1955, 14,666 vessels of all nations with net tonnage of 115,756,000 transited the Suez Canal. British ships are the chief customers.

The Suez Canal and the area that surrounds it is also of fundamental strategic importance. They lie at a crossroads of three continents and separate Asia from Africa. The canal gives access to vital strategic materials, especially the oil of the Middle East. For Britain, it shortens the Cape of Good Hope passage from London to Bombay from 12,374 miles to 7,117 miles, to Singapore from 13,314 to 9,392 miles.

The Suez Canal is in a sense indistinguishable from the zone and base areas around it. Theoretically, the canal has always been an international waterway, open to the ships of all nations without discrimination and recognized as such by the Constantinople Convention of 1888. Actually British control of Egypt and later the bases in the Canal Zone bestowed upon Britain military control of the canal, but even before the British evacuation Egypt was able to prevent Israeli ships from transiting the canal.

The Canal Zone area has long been a strategic focus of the Middle East; its air bases and communications networks were the hub of the area and, until the recent hauling down of the British flag, the Canal Zone was the main focus of British power throughout the Middle East. British evacuation created a vacuum of power, which Egypt is now trying to fill.

The final strategic meaning of the nationalizing of the internationally owned Suez Canal Company cannot yet be predicted. The company which operated the canal was an Egyptian joint-stock corporation with principal offices in Paris. Its stock was owned all over the world, but a big bloc—44 per cent—was owned by the British Government.

If the canal remains open and is operated as before there will be a major economic change—particularly a loss to the stockholders unless Nasser compensates them for the nationalization he has decreed. But this economic sleight-of-hand would have little immediate strategic meaning unless Nasser's emotional chauvinism goes completely out of bounds—something that cannot be entirely ruled out.

The Suez Canal is not absolutely vital to the West economically or strategically as World War II showed. Its importance has increased owing to the development of the Middle Eastern oil fields, but pipelines from those fields to the Mediterranean make it possible for some tanker tonnage to by-pass Suez. And the longer voyage around the Cape of Good Hope can be sustained for some time if essential.

Nevertheless, a number of nasty consequences could result from Nasser's sudden and emotional move. The Egyptians now have the only physical force in the actual Canal Zone area; in a physical sense they control the canal. They could (1) keep the canal open, but raise the tolls considerably; (2) reduce or delay canal shipping; (3) close the canal to their enemies—and specifically to all ships carrying supplies to Israel; and (4) if threatened, sabotage or block the canal.

But Egypt is particularly vulnerable to economic pressure and if she does reduce any major volume of canal shipping she will be cutting off her nose to spite her face, for she is counting on canal revenues to help finance ambitious economic schemes, including the Aswan Dam. [See "Egypt's Aswan Dam Project," Section III, below.]

Moreover strategists have already discounted to some extent the canal's importance in time of major war; it can be blocked so easily by mines, A-bombs or other means that no strategic calculation can count upon its use.

The most mischievous strategic consequences of Nasser's action, therefore, would seem to be local—in the Middle East,

North African area—though more widespread in the economic field in Britain, France and elsewhere.

Nasser's recklessness, preceded by many Western mistakes, weaknesses and short-sightedness, have now clearly aligned the West against him. France has at length denounced Egypt—the psychological and political fountainhead of much of her difficulty in North Africa. Israel benefits emotionally, psychologically and politically in the unstable Middle East equation. And chauvinistic Pan-Arabism will become more explosive than ever.

NEGOTIATIONS ON THE SUEZ CANAL [9]

For sixty-eight years a nine-power convention guaranteed [that the Suez] canal would be kept open "at all times and for all powers." When Gamal Abdel Nasser of Egypt seized the canal [on July 21, 1956], he, in effect, moved to wipe the international guarantee off the books. . . .

Colonel Nasser's nationalization decree set off the Suez crisis . . . [and] war clouds gathered. Britain and France, dependent upon the canal for oil transport and already embroiled with Cairo on other Mideast issues, dispatched troops and flattops. Cairo shot back defiance. Only after a hasty trip to London by Secretary Dulles did the Big Three decide to call . . . [a] London conference . . . [on the issue].

Their purpose was to mobilize moral force for internationalization of the canal. To this end they could count on the backing of eleven other Western countries invited to London. But Egypt spurned an invitation, and so did Greece, at odds with Britain over Cyprus. Seven Afro-Asian nations headed by India wanted canal passage assured but were as much concerned to tell the West: "Hands Off Egypt," as President Sukarno of Indonesia put it. And the Soviet Union, interested in passage through the canal, was at least equally interested in making bad blood between the West and the Afro-Asian countries.

Just such a split seemed to be shaping up at the fourth day of the conference. . . . Secretary Dulles presented a Big Three plan for an international Suez Canal Board charged with full authority for the "operation, maintenance and development of the canal." Krishna Menon of India proposed nearly the opposite— that a "consultative body of user interests be formed . . . without prejudice to Egyptian ownership and operation [of the canal]."

Compromise Agreement

[Then] Mr. Dulles met with Pakistan's Foreign Minister Hamidul Huq Chowdhury, and hammered out a compromise. The revised wording merely added emphasis to Egypt's status as a sovereign nation, "giving," as Mr. Chowdhury explained it, "due weight to the emotions and patriotic sentiments of peoples who have recently achieved independence." But it proved acceptable to Turkey, Ethiopia and Iran as well as Pakistan. . . . The compromise was approved by all countries except India, Russia, Indonesia and Ceylon. It . . . [provided] in main, that there should be established by a convention negotiated with Egypt:

A Suez Canal Board [responsible] for operating, maintaining and developing the canal. . . . The members of the board, in addition to Egypt, would be other states chosen in a manner to be agreed upon from among the states party to the convention. . . .

There remained the question of broaching the recommendation to Cairo. . . . Mr. Menon and Dmitri Shepilov of Russia argued that sending a committee to present the Dulles proposals to Cairo would be "one-sided." "Dilatory tactics," was Secretary Dulles' comment . . . [and finally] the eighteen nations supporting the Dulles' plan moved to break the procedural tie-up. They named Australian Prime Minister Robert Menzies as chairman and delegates from Ethiopia, Iran, Sweden and the United States to a committee charged with bearing their recommendations to Cairo. After that, as one briefing officer put it later, "there was nothing to do but adjourn." . . .

[At the close of the London Conference it was felt that Colonel Nasser might] be tempted to spurn the eighteen-nation proposals out of hand. Ever since nationalization he has bent every resource to avoid surrendering control of the canal. But Colonel Nasser does not have a free hand. To reject the majority view of the London conference directly would be another slap in the face of the West. It would further strain Egypt's relations with countries on whom she depends heavily for trade and, in the long run, economic aid.

Moreover, there is no certainty Egypt can continue to keep canal traffic running smoothly. About 250 pilots are normally on hand to steer ships through the canal and of that number about 200 are non-Egyptians. Some Western pilots, on home leave when nationalization was announced, have not returned, and Egypt has already been forced to rearrange the convoy system. Britain claimed that Egypt had threatened discrimination against British and French ships, if a pilot slow-down developed. Cairo denied the charge. But it is clear that any breakdown of service would affect all users, turning world opinion against Cairo.

In these circumstances the odds . . . [were] that Colonel Nasser . . . [would] move to bargain. . . . A New York *Times* correspondent long resident in Cairo cabled from London. . . :

Egypt is expected to explain that she cannot negotiate under duress of military threats, and that since she did not recognize the London conference, its proposals are unacceptable as a basis for negotiations. It is thought that Cairo, with backing from Moscow, will ask for a conference of all fifty nations using the Suez Canal.

[Thereafter Egypt refused to accept the proposals of the London conference which were presented to Cairo by a five-nation commission headed by Prime Minister Robert Menzies of Australia. The United States, Britain, and France then proposed that a Users' Association be formed to protect rights of users of the canal, employ pilots, coordinate the canal's traffic, and seek Egyptian cooperation. To this plan Nasser reacted bluntly— claiming that such a proposal was a challenge, the object of which was to bring about a state of war.

Again a London conference was called to discuss the Big Three plan for a Users' Association. It was uncertain, however, whether the Big Three would press the matter as some user nations objected to the new plan. It was also uncertain whether a peaceful outcome of the Suez crisis could be achieved. First the user group would have to test Egyptian reaction to sending a ship through the canal. In the face of continued Egyptian refusal to come to terms on the canal, the Western powers could—short of using force—bypass the canal by sending ships around Africa and thus apply crippling economic pressures against Egypt.

As this book went to press, Egypt, with Soviet backing, had called for a conference, larger than the London group, to meet in Cairo. There was much likelihood, however, that the issues involved in the crisis would be referred to the United Nations by mutual consent.—Ed.]

II. OLD AND NEW FORCES

EDITOR'S INTRODUCTION

It could be argued that the ground, the background and the underground of the Middle East are the three determining factors affecting Middle Eastern affairs today.

At present neither the lands of the Arab countries nor those of the other nations of the area are under wholly productive use for the peoples of those localities. Problems pertaining to land use and land distribution, in fact, form some of the chief issues which both the local governments and outside powers are attempting to deal with. Underground, on the other hand, lie some of the richest oil deposits of the world—again resources not yet serving in any full measure the needs of the vast majority of Middle Easterners. But the lands of the Middle East and the underground petroleum wealth also figure in the power struggle on the world stage. For it is almost a cliché that the Middle East lies at the crossroads of three continents—no less strategically vital in the air age than when Alexander the Great stalked eastward to India. The oil supplies below the surface far surpass those available to the Soviet Union and are crucial to Western European industry and the free world defense machine.

The background of the Middle Eastern peoples—their histories, religions and ways of life—also profoundly affect current developments. Some aspects of both the old and the new background forces playing upon the thought and action of these peoples are surveyed in this section. Space limits this discussion largely to the Arab world and thus the first selection deals mainly with the Arabs' past. It touches briefly, however, on the effect contemporary schools of thought are having on the Arab nations. In the article which follows a case is made out that people in masses—the mob—play a decisive role in present-day Middle Eastern affairs. The rather disheartening experience, from a Western viewpoint, with democracy, which various Middle Eastern states have adopted as a form of government from time to time, is dealt with next. Not as a matter of balance, but by way of setting up the danger signals, the more recent appeal of communism is explained in the last article.

Obviously, in such brief compass much about the deep-seated patterns of the various societies of the Middle East must be left out. Turkey's past and its more recent revival, the emergent Pakistan, the Christian state of Lebanon, Iran and Israel all vary greatly from the Arab countries as they themselves show marked differences, for example, Syria as contrasted with the fabulous Saudi Arabia. But where history is still alive and religion a way of life unknown in the West, the background of Middle Easterners necessarily conditions today's conduct. Understanding of this background inevitably calls for extensive reading beyond these few articles.

THE ARABS' PAST [1]

Since the trade routes of Europe, Asia and Africa were funneled for centuries through their home, it was natural that the Arabs should become middlemen and should set up markets and "merchant republics" on the caravan routes. In one of these caravan stops, Mecca, on the spice route from Damascus to Yemen, Mohammed was born in 571 A.D. Like a number of great figures of history, Mohammed was the son of a noble family which had fallen on lean days; so young Mohammed went to work as a commercial agent. At the age of 25 he married a rich widow, many years his senior, and his middle age was spent in leisure and comfort. He won respect as a man who was a successful and honest businessman among businessmen. Then, when he was over 40 and, in the view of his fellows, should have been settled in the ways of the community, Mohammed received his call to lead his people to the worship of *the*

[1] From *What the Arabs Think*, pamphlet by William R. Polk, fellow of the Rockefeller Foundation, and W. Jack Butler, head of public relations division for an American oil company in the Middle East. (Headline Series no 96) Foreign Policy Association. November-December 1952. p7-18. Reprinted by permission.

one God and to warn them of Judgment Day. So he turned
from his former life and began to preach what was to become
the religion of Islam. .

At first Mohammed drew his followers mainly from the
slaves and poor people of Mecca, and for ten years he and they
were a persecuted and despised group. By 622 A.D. the Meccans
had about decided to rid themselves of this troublemaker. In
that year Mohammed and his followers quit Mecca and mi-
grated to the town of Medina (about 200 miles to the north),
where Mohammed became a ruler. It is from the date of migration, the *Hegira*, when Mohammed left Mecca and began to
rule a state and Islam began to show signs of worldly success
and power, that the years of the Moslem lunar calendar are
dated. Unlike the Judaic-Christian growth in adversity, suffering
and persecution, Islam was almost from the beginning a religion
of rulers and of visible worldly success. The days of persecution
for the Moslems were short, and the years of victory were spec-
tacularly brilliant. In less than a hundred years after Mohammed's death, the Moslem Empire stretched from southern France
to India; and because the Arabs were successful, it was natural
that Islam should get the credit. Submission to the will of God
paid off in this world, and the word "Islam" came to mean
success.

The second aspect of Islam which conditions modern Arab
thought is the fact that quite early in its development Islam
became at once a religion, a state and a way of life. Then and
now, it is difficult to make a convenient separation between
secular and religious affairs. As yet, Islam has had nothing comparable with the Protestant Reformation and remains relatively
impervious to the secular ideas which have come into the modern
Arab world. Western ideas and ways coexist with, but have not
been assimilated into, Islam.

Briefly, then, Islam is a difficult religion to modify formally.
Also, and this is of great importance for the modern Arabs,
Islam was developed in such an atmosphere of success that it
offers little of the succor many of the modern Arabs desperately
crave.

The "Long Sleep"

Soon after the death of Mohammed, the Moslem Empire had expanded far beyond the scope of the laws and practices he had adopted in Mecca and Medina; so the Arabs were forced to learn from their subject peoples. In particular, they took over a large part of the personnel and practices of the Byzantine Empire and gradually began to use Greek methods of thought and to absorb Greek ideas. These, on the one hand, and the growth of mysticism on the other posed far-reaching philosophical problems that acted as a stimulus to the great period of Moslem culture. But the great period was to be relatively short and was followed by the "long sleep" of Islam and of the Arabs. Because many of the visible and invisible aspects of the modern Arab world result from this "long sleep" it is important to understand how it came about and what effect it has had.

In the first place, the enormous wealth and luxury that came with their empire led the Arabs to rest on their laurels. They imported Central Asian Turks as mercenaries to serve in their armies and soon found that the Turks were running *them* as well as the armies. Also, the intellectual fermentation precipitated by Greek thought and logic ended in the complete triumph of state-supported orthodoxy. The rationalists were purged, and orthodoxy was securely clamped on the Arabs' minds. . . .

Thus, inwardly Islam was losing its vitality, was retreating into its past, and its first citizens, the Arabs, were being replaced by Turks and Persians when the great blow fell from Central Asia. In 1258 the Mongol armies of Genghis Khan, under his grandson Hulagu Khan, captured and destroyed Baghdad, at that time the major city, capital and cultural center of the Islamic Empire, killing 800,000 people in a week of terror. Next, Hulagu destroyed the Syrian city of Aleppo, putting 50,000 of its citizens to the sword. The "peace" of a graveyard followed for 150 years until Timur Leng (Tamerlane) took up where Hulagu had left off, killing and burning what little had come to life in the intervening years. In 1400 Timur destroyed Aleppo and in 1401, Damascus, killing or carrying off into slavery all of the learned men and skilled craftsmen and reducing the schools and libraries to ruins. To this day the Arab world has not fully recovered from these blows.

Four centuries of Ottoman Turkish domination followed. In spite of some merits in its early years, the Ottoman Empire became in the Arab world a highly organized form of robbery and suppression. Every movable object of value which the Mongols had not destroyed or which had been rebuilt was drained into the Ottoman capital. . . .

So the Arab world was bled white, was suppressed into ignorance, and was politically cowed to the point that government as such is still an object of suspicion or even terror to many Arabs.

Finally, as though these were not enough, another anesthetic was administered to the Arabs by Vasco da Gama in 1498. Reaching India by sea, da Gama enormously stimulated European trade and thereby plunged the middlemen of the land caravan routes of the Middle East into a depression which lasted into the nineteenth century.

Before the Arab world went to sleep, the Arabs formed their impression of the West. Europe was just emerging from the Dark Ages while Islam was at the pinnacle of its success. The Arab world with its many schools and libraries was the center of culture and learning to which Europeans turned for inspiration. The first book published in England, in 1477, was based on an Arabic original, and the great Roger Bacon advised his students that they could do no better than to leave England to study with the Arabs. The Crusades, which had made such a profound impression on Europe, did little more than to confirm the Arab opinion of Western barbarianism. Then, to the Arabs came the long period of orthodoxy, destruction and stagnation; and to the West, the Renaissance, the Reformation and the French Revolution. In 1798, in the wake of the French Revolution, there landed in Egypt the finest army and a hundred of the leading scholars of Europe under the command of Napoleon. The kitten of the eleventh and twelfth centuries' Crusaders, whose antics had merely amused the Arabs, had become in the nineteenth century a Napoleonic lion, which fell upon the sleeping Arabs and methodically began to devour them.

The School of Modern Thought

The nineteenth century is the school of the modern Arab's mind. His reactions to the events of the mid-twentieth century grow directly out of the events and impressions of the years 1798-1920. . . .

The first reaction to Napoleon's invasion, which revealed European superiority, was essentially the same as the earlier reaction to the success of Mohammed. The Arabs sought the cause of success and identified themselves with it. They supposed that the reasons for Western superiority lay in Western habits and customs. Should those be copied and followed, success would surely again return to the Arabs. So, following the lead of Mohammed Ali, ancestor of the recently deposed King Farouk, a school of thought has developed which favors the slavish copying of the West.

Copying the West

Mohammed Ali, an Albanian in the service of the Turks, was sent to Egypt to help expel the French; but he had bigger plans. By 1805 he had managed to seize power in this province of the Ottoman Empire, and in the face of Turkish opposition had to find a way of maintaining his position. He had observed how easily the modern French army had defeated the forces of the Sultan; and, he reasoned, to make himself secure against the same foe he needed the same weapons, a modern military machine and the economy to support it. So he began to lure back to Egypt some of Napoleon's old officers to train soldiers, and European technicians to create a modern industry to support and equip an army. Then he sent to Europe groups of Egyptian students to be trained to man his government and to run the new economy. By 1839 the Egyptian army numbered almost 200,000 men and, to Europe's amazement, embarked on a sizable imperialistic scheme by conquering the Sudan, the Arabian Peninsula, Syria and most of Anatolia. It was advancing on the Ottoman capital itself when the alarmed great powers obliged Mohammed Ali to order a retreat and forced him to break up his control over the Egyptian economy, thus nipping in the bud a Middle Eastern state which had already become what Japan was later to be in the Pacific, the student par excellence of the West.

It would be incorrect to read nationalism into Mohammed Ali's movement. To Mohammed Ali, Egypt was simply a base of operations and a source of the raw materials of power. As far as Mohammed Ali was concerned, except for a set of accidental circumstances, he might just as well have been in Syria, Albania or Turkey itself. However, his activity laid the groundwork for nationalism, and his student missions together with the schools of foreign missionaries, which he tolerated, brought into the Arab world many ideas, including nationalism, from Europe. Mohammed Ali planted the seed, and forty years after his death a very different sort of movement began. Under an Egyptian army officer of peasant origin, Arabi Pasha, Egypt underwent its first national revolt.

The revolt was crushed the year it began, 1882, by a British Army invasion from the Suez Canal zone and a Royal Navy bombardment of Alexandria, but the episode provided a tragic and heroic incident to be glorified by succeeding generations of nationalists. . . .

At the turn of the century political nationalism was propagated in Egypt by a small circle around Mustafa Kamil, a French-educated young lawyer. Following Kamil came groups of nationalists, including the great Sa'ad Zaghlul of Egypt, which gained in popularity and power right up to the moment that they managed to win a measure of independence. Their reason for existence was the presence of foreigners in the Arab world, and their aim was to expel them; so they, like Mohammed Ali before them, sought to discover the causes of Western success. They saw the West in a different way; whereas Mohammed Ali had copied armies, they thought that the source of Western success was the feeling of belonging to a country or nation.

Disillusionment with the West

These attempts to discover the "secret" of Western power acted as great stimuli to Arab thinking. Gradually, however, the Arabs have grown disillusioned with the West. Wars and depressions, together with the more obvious shortcomings of Western culture, have turned away some, while others have been even more disillusioned with their copies of Western institutions. Few of these copies have flourished on an alien soil. Many Arabs, moreover, grasped only the more external aspects of Western thought and expected from it what it could not produce. . . . This turn from the West has recently been accelerated by the material decline of the European imperial powers and by their obvious inability to solve their own problems. Their show of weakness quite naturally is raising the question, "Does the secret of success, after all, really lie in the Western way of life?"

The answer, say the numerous Moslem revival groups in the Arab states, is No. On a number of social and political questions, which only recently have confronted Islam, they are unsure just what the answers are, but increasingly they are looking for the answers in their view of Islam rather than in the West. As yet, these groups have gained power in the Arab world only in Saudi Arabia and to a lesser extent in Libya, and in Pakistan outside of the Arab world, but they form powerful blocs in Egypt, Syria and, to some extent, in Iraq. But in power or out, the very existence of this will to return to a pre-Western and, in some ways, anti-Western way of life is bound to affect considerably the thought and actions of all of the modern Arabs.

To many foreigners living in the Arab world one of its most confusing aspects is the fact that many groups which in Western eyes appear totally in opposition work together. Even more confusing is the fact that in the opinions of one man are often united two totally contradictory views on what, to a Westerner, appears to be one subject

The reason for both of these confusing aspects is that Arabs make a sharp division between domestic and foreign politics, and that to a large degree their political thought is still oriented toward foreign affairs. Westerners, by contrast, tend to divide issues on a domestic plane; so, many Westerners express surprise when a "reactionary" Moslem sincerely co-operates with a "revolutionary" Communist. At this stage of the development of the area the essential thing for both the fervent Moslem and the fervent Communist is to get the Western powers out of the Arab world. The fact that once the "foreigners" have departed, the two will surely not agree on domestic matters is only beginning to mar their relationship because only in the last five years has much thought been given to domestic changes. For almost everyone except the largely unpopular landowner governments the central goal has been to change the present state of affairs, and on one thing everyone is agreed, the foreigners must go. . . .

The Arabs are no more homogeneous than any other people, and there are fundamental differences of outlook and opinion among the several main groups of people in the Arab states. . . .

The vast majority of the Arabs are farmers (fellaheen) and herdsmen. As yet, they are so bound by the fetters of poverty, ignorance and disease (to translate the Arabic phrase) that they have been unable to show many signs of political life. To date they have expressed almost no political thought, as they have been unable to do more than barely keep alive. To Westerners their poverty is far beyond the scope of anything known in the West as poverty. As a noted British economist put it, "They have no standard of living . . . ; anything less would be death.". . . To talk to them in terms of democracy or freedom is to mock them; for them the basic question is life or death—not how life can be led. Thus, they say little; yet they act as a sort of brake on the political thought of the other groups and constitute a big question mark about the political future of the area.

Closest, perhaps, to the people are the pious Moslems and religious men of the older generation. Islam has no clergy in the Christian sense, yet it has developed numerous brotherhoods, religious orders, and officials who circulate among the people as teachers, readers of the Koran, and judges. For them Islam is the touchstone of all thought, and they form the cadres of the various Moslem revival movements. Usually their thought is quite conservative by Western standards, but they are effectively linked with the fellaheen because they are the teachers in the village schools and because they alone have something of a message of hope for the downtrodden peasantry.

Who Are the Leaders?

More distant, yet intellectually more concerned with the plight of the fellaheen, are the Western-educated men and women of the younger generation who are the doctors, lawyers, professors, engineers and white-collar workers of the Arab world. Their fathers were the nationalists, and they are today's "social nationalists," combining a domestic reform program with nationalism. Certainly they are the most vocal section of the population and to a large extent are bound to be the key to the Arab world's immediate future. . . .

At the top of the social pyramid are the people who profit from the present order. They are the landowners, who predominate in the parliaments of every one of the Arab states except in Egypt, where a military government seems to be replacing them. In many cases they were the radical young nationalists of thirty years ago who won their place in their societies and settled down to enjoy and maintain it. In recent years they have maintained their positions by accepting the support, in some cases armed support, of interested foreign powers and by playing the other groups off against one another. New their power is rapidly declining, and their future in the Arab world is unstable. However, they are still making the decisions of the government of most of the Arab countries, and their decisions are the laws of most of the Arabs.

PEOPLE ON THE MOVE—THE MOB [2]

The recipe for making a mob is always the same: "Take a cluster of mean streets; fill with idle or semi-employed people; sprinkle with raw notions of social betterment; top with hunger, or despair at rising prices; stir and bring to boil." Of these ingredients the most important are the unemployment and the cramped quarters, for they insure that the rumor which sets men moving reaches the maximum of ears in the minimum of time.

They apply in any continent—Europe and America as well as Asia and Africa. The years in which the historic Paris mob swayed policy were before Haussman built the boulevards. "Go to the mob" was the theme of *"Mein Kampf,"* yet Hitler could not use it to stir his storm until he was able to profit by the soaring unemployment of 1931, 1932 and 1933.

So in Cairo in January 1952, it was from the teeming slums of the Wasa'a and the Bulaq that the mob was roused to wreck the shops full of goods it could not buy. In Baghdad the same crowd can be mustered from behind the mud walls of the shanties beyond the bund (they live on the wrong side of the levee that checks the Tigris flood). Of the larger Middle Eastern capitals only Damascus, with its wide streets and a population firmly rooted in the busy peasantry of its fertile oasis, is free from mobs of classic make-up. In a word, the crowd that is swaying policy in the Middle East today is a town proletariat, not a peasant jacquerie.

It is whipped into being by the hotfoot messenger who whispers, or maybe shouts, that innocents have been murdered, a shrine violated, or unclean fat mixed by infidel suppliers into some staple food. Sometimes it will watch passively while demolitions proceed. At that stage it is a collection of reasonable individuals, ready to puncture tension with a burst of laughter at the comment of some wag. Then someone throws a

[2] From "Key Force in the Middle East—The Mob," by Elizabeth Monroe, writer on the Middle East for the London *Economist*. New York *Times Magazine*. p 13+. August 30, 1953. Reprinted by permission.

bottle. There is a pause like the hush before a thunderclap. Maybe nothing follows. But maybe the storm breaks and mass hysteria sets in. In a few seconds men that were separate beings have become a solid united mass, yelling, throwing missiles, running twenty and thirty abreast and flecked with saliva, toward fresh targets, capable of any violence and reckless of the consequences.

Second only to the slums as a source of raw material are the classroom and the campus. Any astute Arab politician takes care to time unpopular announcements so that they fall during academic vacation: this is the technique of, for instance, Nuri Pasha of Iraq. Less responsible leaders, particularly in Egypt in the past, have deliberately drawn youths away from their studies in order to heighten mob pressure.

In Cairo, if a religious issue is involved, or can be trumped up, the student mob includes the theological students of the Azhar University—the world's most famous center of Moslem teaching. Most of these are pauper sons of devout peasant families on whom the hopes of an inarticulate home are pinned. But the student bulk, civvy-suited and tarboosh-hatted, comes from Government schools and Europeanized homes; aged from twelve into the twenties, the youths are fired by the excitements that stir any lawless junior. They are set for a spree, and for the sense of power that comes from keeping a cosh [loaded bludgeon] in one's pocket or grenades inside school desks. Like the slum crowd, they can be whipped in a moment from mere noisiness into a frenzy of rage and despair.

Shouting mobs are a long-standing feature of the Middle Eastern scene. Sometimes the demonstrators have been antiforeign, sometimes the paid agents of opposition parties bent on stirring trouble for their political rivals. Between wars when they were familiar chiefly in Egypt (Iran was, in those days, clamped under a dynamic tyranny of the Shah's father) they were noisy and sometimes dangerous, but they were always the servants—never the masters—of the politicians who hired them to shout against Britain or against a rival.

In those days anyone who troubled to count heads could calculate the cost of a mob almost to a piaster. They performed like so many sheep. Their synthetic anger could even be checked if not cured by anyone with sufficient presence of mind to play on their sense of humor. Old Cairo inhabitants recall an occasion when the then Chief of Police, Russell Pasha, mastered a potential riot at the funeral of a political "martyr" by touching the palm of the corpse's hand with his cigarette to be rewarded with a yell to wake the dead, and the crowd dissolved in laughter.

Today no money stimulus is necessary and no laughter is brooked. What used to be a herd has become a wolf pack. The composition of the mob of the 1950's is multiple, but the elements fuse because all are fired with the same new conception of life.

This change of nature does not mean that an ignorant and gullible mass has all of a sudden become sophisticated and constructive or that it has coherent views as to what should happen next. . . .

The Middle Eastern demonstrator has only recently awakened from a sleep of centuries and from the lethargy born of ignorance that any better way of life was to be had. Today he is as unlettered as he always was but he knows what he does *not* want. He does not want the life he has been used to leading in squalor and disease and without hope of a living wage and he does not want rulers who promise him better standards and then fail to alter his lot. The key to his change of outlook is his sudden grasp of the fact that misery is not inevitable.

This revelation has come to him in various ways. The popular belief that he learned it only from Russian propagandists is by no means correct. Like all people who cannot read, your Eurasian or Arab is impressed much less by what he hears than by what he sees. Thus, while Tudeh (Iran's Communist organization) pamphlets and speakers have done their bit toward waking him up they have probably not been so potent in influence as the glimpses he has had on Western living standards and well-being. These glimpses first caught his attention

during the Western invasion of all Middle Eastern countries
during World War II—not only the military invasion but an
oil company one.

Then he saw men, who to him were the common man—
Tommies and GI's and drillers and riveters—eating good meals
and wearing good clothes. He got employment from their masters and the good money they paid attracted him toward the
towns. It caused him to cluster round Teheran and Baghdad
and Cairo in the hateful misery of tin towns and in greater dis-
comfort even than before; simultaneously it awakened his appetite for better things.

Helping to stir his consciousness was a change in the
upper classes. The fact that he was becoming discontented did
not entirely escape the rich landlord politicians of the Middle
East. For several years after the war they sought to assuage
this discontent by seven-year plans and promises of jobs and
housing. Particularly in Iran and in Egypt under the Wafd
[the nationalist party formed in 1918 by Sa'ad Zaghlul] these
promises failed to materialize. Simultaneously these awakening
proletariats saw their rich men behaving more ostentatiously
than in the past.

They saw war profiteers among their own people making
gains while poor men went hungry. They saw these profits
transformed into ways of life much more visibly removed from
their own than those of the old-time rich: new thoughts set
in as the Pashas replaced their shuttered homes and walled
seclusion with open, modern villas and their horses—which
had been not so different from the poor man's donkey—with
Cadillacs and Packards.

They heard that foreign oil companies were paying their
rulers good money but as the only sign of this (except on the
actual oil fields, which are everywhere far removed from the
capital) they beheld an invasion of well-dressed, well-paid
foreigners. They saw Point Four staffs bustling round in trucks
with bright American labels but as the immediate outcome of
this influx knew only that house rents had soared beyond the
range of local salaries. They no longer needed to be prompted

or bribed to demonstrate. They now burned with resentment which they were ready to work off not only against the West but against any of their own leaders who had preached a better deal and then failed to practice it.

The Middle Eastern mob of today, purposeful and so full of dumb resentment that it can change within seconds from a collection of separate human beings into a mad thing, is no longer out for simple ends, such as loot or hire at a few piasters. Pouring through the bazaar it will tear booty to pieces, hacking into clothing and shoe stores and, though itself ragged and barefoot, rending cloth, tearing uppers apart with teeth and nails, and spiking soles with its staves.

The first mob display of this new kind took place in 1948 in Iraq. At the time it was hardly recognized as such because its immediate cause was a familiar one—a protest at the new defense treaty with Britain. Its overtones were the familiar anti-British parrot cries. Yet it was equally fired by other impulses. There had been a bad harvest; grain stood at twenty times its pre-war cost; certain politicians were known to be hoarding it against a further rise in price. An undertone of the affair was a protest at the callousness of Iraq's rich rulers.

In Cairo in January 1952, "Black Saturday" exposed the change beyond the shadow of a doubt, for the main feature of the day was the organized destruction of the premises and perquisites of the rich. . . . Again in Baghdad . . . [in November 1952] British and American officers were targets for attack, but the mob's greatest resentment was against its own Pasha rulers.

In Teheran . . . the same symptoms have been discernible. . . .

"Mob" is short for *mobile vulgus*—a people on the move. Whether it moves, out of control, toward anarchy or, in control, toward unprecedented social changes, now wholly depends upon the character and grip of . . . [new leaders in the Middle East. But] success would call for a second transformation in the nature of the mob. The first was from herd into pack, the second would need to be from pack into hive.

THE EXPERIENCE WITH DEMOCRACY [3]

Democracy is one of the magic words of our time, with a wide range of different meanings in different parts of the world. In the Middle East too the word has been used in a number of different senses, ranging from parliamentary government to royal condescension. During the last hundred years, however, there has been in the countries of the Middle East a real attempt to apply our kind of democracy, with constitutional government, elected legislatures, and civil rights. Today in most of the Middle East these democratic regimes are in a state of visible collapse. . . . Only in Turkey, Israel, and Pakistan does democratic government seem to be developing with any reasonable prospect of success. The second and third may be excluded from present consideration as having entirely different backgrounds; Israel because of its predominantly immigrant population, Pakistan because of the long preparatory period of imperial peace and the quite different cultural and political background of its people. Democracy in Turkey, however, a Middle Eastern and Islamic country which has much in common with the other countries of the Middle East, presents a striking contrast. . . .

For the greater part of its history the political experience of Islam has been limited to autocratic rule. Not until the end of the eighteenth century and the beginning of the nineteenth, when the doctrines of the French Revolution and other movements arising out of it first began to percolate to the Middle East, did democratic ideas in the modern sense first reach the Islamic world. The impact was immediate and striking, and by the early twentieth century not only the westward-looking liberals but even many of the orthodox religious leaders were paying at least lip-service to democracy, and showed their recognition of the power of the democratic idea by claiming it, along with evolution and most of the other innovations of the nineteenth century, as an Islamic revelation contained in the Koran.

[3] From "Democracy in the Middle East—Its State and Prospects," by Bernard Lewis, Professor of Islamic History, University of London. *Middle Eastern Affairs.* 6:101-7. April 1955. Reprinted by permission.

The Middle Eastern interest in democracy was not purely theoretical. There were also practical attempts to introduce this form of government into Middle Eastern countries. . . .

The process began more than a century and a half ago, when the armies of Napoleon and the ideas of the French revolution awoke the peoples of the Middle East from their long slumber to a painful awareness of their own weakness and relative backwardness. . . .

Nationalism and liberalism were in the European air at that time—and both meant the end of the traditional Islamic order. In place of the theocratic Moslem society, in which social grouping is determined by religious affiliation, there came the new and disruptive Western idea of the nation, as a group of people bound together by country, language and origin, and entitled to political sovereignty. In place of the Sultan—wielding autocratic power as viceregent of God upon earth and upholder of the Divine Law—came the western paraphernalia of constitutions and parliaments, parties, programs—and politicians, elections and newspapers and the rest—all very pleasant for the small group of Western-educated intellectuals who operated them, but completely meaningless to the great mass of the Moslem population. . . .

And . . . today this great experiment has obviously failed. The parliaments and the constitutions are all collapsing, and most countries, if they have not already done so, seem to be on the point of formally abandoning democracy. One may well stop to ask why.

Some causes are obvious. The reforms were precipitate, carried through at far too rapid a pace, without due regard to the conditions in which they were promulgated. They were superimposed from outside, and were irrelevant to events actually occurring in Middle Eastern society at the time. A political system taken over ready-made from another society must fail in many respects to correspond to the different strains and stresses of that to which it is applied. . . .

In a long period of tranquility, the peoples of the Middle East might perhaps have succeeded in adapting these borrowed institutions to their own traditions and way of life; but no such period was vouchsafed to them. The pressure of internal and still more external events left no time or opportunity for experiment and adaptation, and the imported machinery, handled by unskilled operators, broke under the strain or fell into disrepair. Among political leaders the idealism of the first reformers gave way to disappointment, disappointment to frustration, and frustration to a cynicism and opportunism that outraged the moral and religious senses of the Moslem masses and brought the whole concept of democracy into disrepute.

This tide of reaction against western political institutions met and was swollen by the surging wave of hatred against the West generally. It is our complacent habit in the West to assume that our institutions are in all respects superior to those of Oriental societies, and that any change in those societies in the direction of a greater resemblance to our institutions is necessarily an improvement. In fact it is not always so. Westernization has brought many great and self-evident benefits to the Middle East—but it has also wrought great injuries, and, human nature being what it is, it is the latter that have received most attention. One of the most important of these is the social and political formlessness of so many oriental countries. In the traditional Islamic society there was an accepted system of social and political functions, loyalties, and responsibilities. Admittedly, that system was in decay, as was the whole society—but still it worked, and was generally accepted and understood. Most of the damage was done, not by Western rulers and imperialists, but by hasty and energetic native reformers who carried through their westernizing reforms with a ruthlessness and a precipitancy in striking contrast with the cautious conservatism of most imperialist authorities. In the event, they turned out to have destroyed better than they built. While their Western innovations often proved superficial and impermanent, their destruction of the old system of social bonds and obligations was final, and left a gap that has not yet been filled. These changes, and the many economic and social upheavals that accompanied them, have unleashed a great wave of hostility against the West and all that came out of it. In different classes and levels of society it finds different forms of expression—in different areas it is connected with different specific grievances—but for most people it takes the form of a generalized resentment against the alien forces that have dislocated their whole way of life. In the West it is usual to deride Oriental parliaments and elections, but in the Orient these are regarded as Western institutions, and their failure as a failure of the West—as yet another grievance against the West.

Nor can the West disclaim all responsibility. There is a case to be made for and against imperial rule as a stage in political evolution, and the stability of the states that emerged from the former Indian Empire suggests that the imperial peace was not without its merits. But there is little that can be said in defense of the half-hearted, pussy-footing imperialism encountered by most of the peoples of the Middle East—an imperialism of inter-ference without responsibility, which would neither create nor permit stable and orderly government.

These difficulties, augmented by the well-known economic upheavals and political grievances of the Middle East, suffice in themselves to explain the failure of a form of government which, as in the nineteenth century, though with the reverse effect, is associated in the public mind with its Western countries of origin. But it may be useful to carry our enquiry beyond present cir-cumstances and to try and see how far the nature of Islamic political and social traditions will favor or discourage the eventual emergence of democratic government.

Despite the traces of nomadic freedom surviving in classical Islamic legal theory, the political traditions and experience of Islam are almost entirely autocratic. The citizen owed, as a re-ligious duty, absolute and unquestioning obedience to the sov-ereign, and had no rights other than that of living the good Moslem life. The sovereign was bound to observe the Holy Law and to make possible the good Moslem life, but apart from that he could do as he pleased. Islamic theory has never recognized any source of authority other than either God or power. The pious régime—that of the Caliph—derives its authority from God. The only alternative source of authority is power—material and effective power, which may however receive a sort of *post facto* divine approval if the holder of power recognizes and maintains the Holy Law. . . . All authority is thus personal. Islamic law does not recognize corporate persons, and Islamic history does not show any elected bodies or corporate authorities. Thus there was no state but only a ruler, no court but only a judge, no city but only a conglomeration of families, quarters, and guilds.

On the other hand there are certain elements in Islam which provide a possible basis for democratic development. One of these is the traditional tolerance of Islam in both race and religion, which is perhaps one of the cardinal virtues of Islamic society. That does not mean to say that Islam has been entirely free from race prejudice or that it has ever conceded equality to followers of other religions in the Islamic state. Its record however, on the whole, in these matters, is infinitely better than that of any society to the west of it. Even in the greater test of toleration of heresy the record of Islamic tolerance is extremely good. . .

Some features of Islamic society which are often adduced by romantics and apologists as "fundamentally democratic" would probably be better described as equalitarian. There is, however, a great deal of social democracy in Islam, both in theory and in practice. . . . This social democracy, though it has never found any political expression, may yet serve as a basis on which some form of political democracy could be built.

More directly relevant to political life is the Islamic doctrine of the rule of law. The Islamic sovereign, though an autocrat, is no true despot. He is not above the law but is subject to the law no less than the humblest of his slaves. It is true that as a restriction on the autocratic powers of the sovereign this is rather theoretical. For one thing the law itself concedes him almost absolute powers; for another the law provides no machinery for its own enforcement against the will of the sovereign. Nevertheless it is broadly true that Islamic sovereigns, with very few exceptions, have maintained the basic principles of the Islamic law at least as far as was required by the public opinion of their time, and respect for law has remained one of the deepest instincts of Islamic society.

The success of democracy in Turkey requires separate explanation. It is difficult at this early stage to distinguish symptoms from causes, but some features may be noted. One of the most striking is the greater realism and responsibility of the Turks, who feel able to adopt a practical approach to problems and thus to make decisions related to facts and abide by them. Unlike their neighbors, the Turks have always been masters in their own house, and indeed in other peoples' houses too. Their political thinking has in consequence not been bedeviled by the problem of foreign rule and the struggle to end it. The process of westernization and reform has gone very much further in Turkey than in any of the other countries. Turkey's foreign policy has shown much greater awareness of the Russian danger, of which the Turks have long and direct experience. Finally—and perhaps this is the most important of all—the economic and social changes which have taken place since the republic was established have changed the social structure of Turkey and given her a social order that provides a much sounder basis for democratic development. It has often been asserted by critics that many of the economic development projects carried through by Kemal Atatürk and his successors were wasteful and inefficient. This may be so, and it may well be that in purely economic terms they were not worth while. Nevertheless, in the light of subsequent events, it must be agreed that these reforms, however much open to criticism on economic grounds, have wholly justified themselves in terms of their social consequences. I refer especially to the emergence of a new middle class of business men, managers, technicians, and the like, self-confident and self-assertive, increasingly intolerant of the older ruling groups of civil servants, landowners, and military men, and increasingly assertive of their own rights. It is this group, more than any other, that has made possible the working of orderly parliamentary government in Turkey, and it is at least arguable that until such groups appear in the other countries of the Middle East there is little prospect there of an orderly development of free institutions.

THE APPEAL OF COMMUNISM [4]

It is possible to discern four different periods in the history of Middle Eastern communism. In 1919-1920 the first Communist groups came into being in Turkey, Palestine, and Egypt. But their efforts were doomed from the outset; the Communists of that era put themselves into deliberate and radical opposition not only to the governments of the day, but also to all political, religious, and social institutions and traditions. They wanted to create proletarian mass parties in countries without an industrial proletariat. They launched a frontal attack against Islam at a time when its hold on the masses was as strong as ever.

By 1923 it was obvious that these attempts had failed. The Communist parties in Turkey and Egypt had ceased to exist; the party in Palestine lingered on precariously without any hope of gaining mass support. Yet it was only in the middle 1930's that a break was made with the "radical" past. This break came as a concomitant of the popular-front tactics of the Comintern in Europe and America; but it was the line which came to stay in the Middle East, with certain important modifications (the change into a "national," "anti-imperialist" front, etc.). Now all radical-socialist demands were dropped, as was the enmity to Islam, and the unwillingness to collaborate with other parties. In countries such as Syria and Iraq, Communist parties grew during that period and attained (in the Levant, at least), a certain importance. Their main competitors at that time were the semi-Fascist groups whose power of attraction was often greater than their own.

It was World War II which brought a great upsurge in Middle Eastern communism. Two of the reasons for this growth in influence were the emergence of the Soviet Union as one of the two great world powers and the downfall of Nazi Germany and Fascist Italy. It is true that World War II also brought economic, and especially industrial, progress to the Middle East, and the consequent emergence of stronger workers' organizations

[4] From Chapter 20, "Conclusions," in *Communism and Nationalism in the Middle East*, by Walter Z. Laqueur, a German-born Israeli and specialist in Middle Eastern affairs, Frederick A. Praeger. New York, 1956. p271-85. Reprinted by permission.

than had existed previously. But it was not the class struggle which gave communism its main impetus, but rather a general feeling that the Middle East was at last beginning to stir after so many years of stagnation. Communist parties made considerable progress in Egypt and Palestine, in the Levant and Iraq, and even in Turkey. The social group most closely connected with communism in all these countries was the intelligentsia. Although there prevailed a feeling among them that things were in motion, the intelligentsia had not attained full political emancipation anywhere in the Middle East.

The fourth period began almost immediately after World War II with the deterioration in the relations between the Arab countries and the West. The popular front of 1935-1937 was now continued as an "anti-imperialist" front in which there was room for all "honest patriots without distinction of class, political, or religious convictions." The Middle East became the testing-ground . . . for all kinds of Communist-front organizations.

Achievements in Turkey and Israel were less spectacular, for several reasons. There was no serious agrarian problem in either country; their Westernization (or modernization) had gone very far; the politically active elite in both countries was, on the whole, more mature; and, last but not least, Russia had been directly threatening Turkey's independence, on the one hand, and had launched a campaign against "cosmopolitans" in Russia and the satellites on the other, which, though discontinued after Stalin's death, was not easily forgotten in Israel. But if there was stability in Turkey and Israel, the political, social, and spiritual crisis in the Arab world had grown rapidly since World War I, and in the vacuum created as the result of the breakdown of tradition, communism rushed in as one of the strongest political competitors for leadership.

The sources of Communist strength are manifold. The decay of Islamic society and its values, together with the absence of liberal and democratic-socialist forces (for which there was little room in the specific conditions of the Middle East), made

Communist success easier than it was in Europe, where it had to face political and spiritual competition. Resistance to communism was confined to retrograde forces, vested interests, and certain religious dignitaries, but there was no opposition to communism among the intelligentsia. Such opposition could have been based only on the defense of freedom and the liberty of the individual, but freedom and liberty were lacking in the Middle East, and where they had existed they were not so highly valued. . . .

Communism in the Middle East has functioned widely as a movement of a middle-class revolt against feudal rule. But this does not mean that the intelligentsia, having attained its political emancipation, will automatically cease to be Communist. . . . They believe probably in the essential goodness of the fellaheen and workers, but they also think them utterly incapable of managing their own affairs; the masses will need the tutelage by the enlightened vanguard for many, many years. In the meantime a revolution will have to take place, and they see no better theory of "revolution from above" than communism. . . . Their Western values have never been more than skin deep. . . . The impact of communism as a technique for modernizing the Middle East, of overcoming its present backwardness in the shortest possible time, is therefore of the greatest importance. Capitalism is identical with imperialist rule, and democracy was something the imperialist powers allegedly practice at home. Democracy was not a militant creed, nor very attractive to them, and it did not provide the answers to many specifically Asiatic questions. . . .

Nationalism in the Middle East is not a force opposed to communism. On the contrary, at the present time it has paved the way for and has collaborated with it. Communism, more often than not, (like nineteenth century liberalism in Europe) had grown up together with nationalism, and for many years a conflict between the two was not considered possible. The meaning of nationalism had been very clear under foreign rule: it was independence, home rule, evacuation of foreign forces. But once independence had been achieved, cynicism and disillusionment took over. . . .

Chances of Communist Success

The numerical strength of Communist parties in the Middle East may not appear impressive to the American or Western European observer.

Egypt	7000-8000	Jordan	1000-2000
Israel	4000-5000	Iraq	3000-5000
Lebanon	8000-10,000	Sudan	1000-1500
Syria	10,000	Turkey	3000

The decisive test, however, is not in figures—above a certain vital minimum, of course—but elsewhere. How strongly rooted is the power of the state? Has the Communist party any serious rivals on the left, or elsewhere? Would it be sufficient for it to conquer a few urban centers? How many sympathizers does the party have, how strong are its "front" organizations? The replies to these (and several other) pertinent questions would obviously differ widely if we compared the situation in some Western European country with that in a Middle Eastern state (apart from Turkey and Israel)—or even with the situation in Russia in 1917. . . .

A dispassionate review of the political trends in the Middle East appears to show that the question of whether or not these countries will become Communist has not yet been decided. But it would also tend to show that there is no reason for undue optimism for the West. It will depend only partly upon events in the Middle East itself, and even if the West were to be wiser politically than it is now in its present dealings in the Middle East, it is doubtful whether this would decisively influence the course of events in the Middle East. It would merely create the prerequisites for success, but no more than that. For the West can give money, can supply agricultural machinery and even jets and tanks, but it cannot provide what is needed most: a competent native elite with a high degree of political maturity. There is little sense in closing one's eyes to the reality; the absence of such a group is the main source of the permanent Middle Eastern crisis—so far as it depends at all on these countries themselves. . . .

The situation in Turkey and Israel is altogether different from the conditions prevailing in the Arab countries; nothing which could possibly happen there would affect developments in the Arab countries. An Arab victory over Israel or an Israeli victory over the Arab states would change little in the trends outlined above; it might, of course, hasten the process of distintegration. Peace between Israel and the Arab countries would be a very welcome stabilizing factor, but it is unlikely in the near future.

What, then, remains to be done by the West? We have stressed time and again that the possibilities of action are fairly limited. Their key is in the hands of the native Arab elites. . . .

Will . . . [the Asian] neutrals defend their own cause? Will they be able to distinguish between social reform and progress and totalitarianism? The Turks will defend their independence because they feel the danger at close quarters; the Arab governments question the very existence of a danger. Some of these countries are ruled by extremely reactionary regimes which see their main task to be the prevention of social progress. All reform movements have been branded "communistic" in these countries and there is hardly reason for surprise that for them the Soviet Union and the Communist party have become the symbol of social justice and progress. It is almost hopeless to try to convince citizens of these countries that they are likely to lose human freedom and basic liberties under communism; they are little afraid of losing what they do not have, anyway.

The obvious course of action for the West would therefore be to support the forces of reform against the reactionary powers who are leading their countries toward catastrophe. Many opportunities have been let slip by in that field. . . .

Need for a Creed

The Middle East is a world in urgent need of a universal message, and this goes, *a fortiori,* for the Middle Eastern intelligentsia. The West has been offering technical aid and Point Four loans, while communism offers a new creed. To paraphrase the late Joseph Schumpeter, technical aid is a poor substitute for the holy grail. Communism's power of attraction as a quasi-religious creed should never be underrated, and it is nowhere so strong as in underdeveloped countries, such as those of the Middle East. In the Soviet Union everybody has a first-hand opportunity to compare ideals with realities: he can see for himself how much social justice and freedom there is in the Soviet and satellite societies. In the countries of the West, much information on Soviet realities is available too, and Leninism has a tough time standing up to competition in the free market of ideas and ideologies. But the intelligentsia of the Middle East gets Leninism pure and unalloyed, and next to nothing is known about Soviet conditions; anyway, the *idea* is the important criterion. They want to receive Leninism as if it had not yet been tried anywhere in the world. . . .

If rapid economic development were the main attraction [communism] would still be a formidable threat. . . . But the religious and ethical elements in communism have been of far greater importance, and must be so at a time when the quest for a universal faith is stronger than ever, with traditional religion sterile and losing appeal. Any attempt to understand the power of attraction of communism in the Middle East which disregards the very existence of its moral concepts and the sources of its religious fervor and ideals is doomed from the outset. But this also goes for all underdeveloped countries and is not an observation specific to the Middle East. What is specific to the Middle Eastern situation is the decline of Islam. We stated at the beginning of this study that for the majority of the intelligentsia of the Arab countries, Islam has ceased to be a living force, and a detailed investigation of whether Islam was aiding or arresting the growth of communism would be a question of a certain speculative interest but of little practical importance—so far as the intelligentsia is concerned. Islam is more important for the masses in the Arab countries, but the authoritarian character of Islamic society, in its state of disintegration even more than in its early stages, makes an easy transition to the Communist ideology a possibility, and in some cases a probability. Traditional Islamic autocracy rests—as Professor Bernard Lewis has pointed out—on three pillars: bureaucracy, the army, and the religious hierarchy.

And it is quite true that in this pattern only the third factor, the religious hierarchy, need be changed in order to prepare the way for a Communist state.

Successful resistance to communism is possible on the basis of a society which is either very developed, or is untouched by what is commonly called civilization. Unfortunately, most Middle Eastern countries are very far from being modern societies, and even farther from achieving an internal balance—but they have proceeded too far from the primitive state to put the clock back. A rational exposition of the mistaken basic tenets of communism presupposes fairly extensive philosophical, psychological, and historical studies of such questions as the nature of man, the will to power, social progress, and kindred subjects, which to the intelligentsia of these countries appear highly abstract if not altogether irrelevant. We shall come to that, they say, but first things first. What we need now, they explain, is economic development to overcome backwardness; later we shall cope with the nature of man. By then, one fears, it will be too late; not perhaps from the point of view of the astronomer's time-scale, but certainly for the social scientist and for the ordinary mortal, who are concerned with the present and the foreseeable future. Nevertheless, it would be wrong to end this study on an entirely pessimistic note. Mob rule and xenophobia in the Middle East have been stressed more than once in the course of this study. . . . Everything now depends on whether these Middle Eastern countries will be able (in a far shorter period) to make the social, political, and economic progress made by the West in a hundred years—and how much time has remained for such vital experimenting. It depends on whether the men will be found to head this immense task, and whether the masses will cooperate; whether the inner strength can be found for an effort unparalleled in many centuries of Middle Eastern history.

III. PROBLEMS AND PROSPECTS

EDITOR'S INTRODUCTION

Several of the most important current problems of the Middle East, and some hopeful prospects for the future, are discussed in this section. The area's general social-economic problems are surveyed in the first selection. This is followed by a very different article concerning problems political and dynastic which exist among the Arab states and showing how these relate to the attempt over the past ten years that has been made to achieve Arab unity in the Arab League.

The article which follows concerns Egypt's proposed Aswan Dam project. In late 1955 and for the first six months of 1956 it appeared that America, Britain and the World Bank might aid Egypt in building the dam. By mid-year, however, both the British and American governments had become suspicious of the pro-Soviet direction which Egyptian foreign policy was taking, and linked to this, because of barter deals with the Communist bloc, suspicious also of the ability of the Egyptian economy to sustain the project. Meantime it was hinted that the Soviet Union was prepared to finance the venture, or at least Egyptian sources so indicated and Soviet statements were at times conflicting. Then the offers from the West were withdrawn and Egypt quickly retaliated by nationalization of the Suez Canal, producing a crisis touched on in the last articles of Sections I and V.

In the discussion about the Jordan River Valley plan quite another problem emerges—one which may eventually give way to great hope. The tragic plight of the Arab refugees is detailed next by an American congressional study mission. This report attempts an objective picture and as such differs from much of the disussion about this unfortunate problem. (Other aspects of the explosive Arab-Israeli conflict are dealt with in Section IV.)

Recent economic problems confronting Turkey, set forth in the next article, raise doubts about the military strength of that nation which is a member of both the Baghdad Pact and the North Atlantic Treaty Organization. In the short article on Cyprus, again, a complex set of factors which seem to operate in any Middle Eastern problem-spot is revealed: British and free-world defense needs, Greek and Turkish aims, and the force of local nationalism. In the final article the problems arising out of Middle Eastern oil exploitation and marketing are related to both United States Government and private business interests.

Problems abound elsewhere and concern a host of other issues in the Middle East, but it has been necessary to omit discussions of many of these. Thus references to Pakistan's part in the Baghdad Pact do not cover dangerous political and economic problems which that new state must meet. Nor is there space to devote to the relations of the Middle East with adjacent areas such as India and North Africa. The tensions between Pakistan and India; the drift toward neutralism on the part of some Arab states, mainly Egypt; and the long-term outlook for Egyptian control over the Suez now that British troops have left their extensive bases there and Egypt has declared the canal nationalized—all of these deserve close attention. Such topics are covered in part by articles and books listed in the bibliography.

THE CHALLENGE OF SOCIAL DISCONTENT [1]

The society of the Near East, at the crossroads of three continents, has been shaped and influenced by myriad currents over the millennia. Its people vary in many respects from one country to another because of differences in their indigenous circumstances and in the foreign influences to which they have been exposed. Yet they share a common experience of centuries of political instability and economic deficiency. This paper will consider the challenge to public responsibility posed by social discontent among the peasants and working classes of the

[1] From "Social Discontent in the Near East: A Challenge to Public Responsibility," by Stephen P. Dorsey, Deputy Director of the Office of Near Eastern Affairs, State Department. *United States Department of State Bulletin.* 32:760-6. May 9, 1955.

predominantly Moslem area extending from the western border of Egypt to the eastern border of Iran.

The period between the two great World Wars, that of partition and the mandates, was one in which the Near Eastern mind, as reflected in the activity of popular leaders, was largely concerned with reunification and independence from Western imperialism, both economic and political. In the decade since the Second Great War and the establishment of independent political units in place of the mandates, the outstanding development may be said to have been the swing of the pendulum toward internal social and economic problems within the new countries. . . .

The Problem and Its Causes

As Sa'id B. Himadeh wrote in the *Near East Journal* in 1951,

The major social problem in the Arab countries of the Middle East is poverty, with its normal concomitants of malnutrition, poor housing, bad sanitation, and disease. It is also the chief problem in the more developed countries, but there are differences in degree, extent, and permanence. Poverty in the Arab countries is so extreme that it often endangers physical subsistence; it embraces a very large proportion of the population; and for the most part it is chronic, not temporary or cyclical as it is in the more advanced countries.

It is extremely difficult to set forth all the basic causes of poverty and unrest in the Arab East and in Iran, properly weighted in depth, proportion, and importance. A brief consideration of some of the principal elements, however, is essential, for without an appreciation of the causes there can be little understanding of the effects or of current measures to root them out.

In the first place, natural resources, with the exception of petroleum, are relatively meager. Water, which may be used as a source of power as well as for irrigation needs, is limited in comparison to the vast stretches of arid land which must remain unproductive without this lifespring. Moreover, the waste of available water supplies, erosion, and salting of cultivable lands contribute to the increasing pressure of population. The effect is intensified by the illiteracy and immobility of labor, and closely related is an outmoded system of land tenure which is as wasteful of manpower as it is of the soil.

State domains in some countries are vast, yet they are subject to various confusing private and tribal claims. Excessive fragmentation and wide separation of small private holdings have increased the difficulty of cultivation. Forms of share tenancy, growing out of extreme inequality of land ownership and a semi-feudal tradition, bring an inadequate share of income to the tenant. Moreover, the insecurity of his tenure and the fact that his rent is a fixed share of the product of his labor discourage the Near Eastern sharecropper from undertaking long-term improvements or even from fertilizing the land. Backward methods of cultivation, the absence generally of credit, except at exorbitant rates, and a lack of farm-market transport facilities, added to marketing systems which tend to benefit the middleman at the expense of the cultivator, contribute to the difficulties of the peasant.

Class Structure

Another heritage from the past is a rigidly stratified class structure separating the small minority of landlords from the peasant masses; the two groups lack channels through which they can communicate concerning the social and economic questions which are vital to the development of the new nations of the Near East and to their peoples. Moreover, during the last few decades the onset of Western industrialization has created a new laboring class—a rudimentary urban proletariat—workers drawn from the countryside surrounding the factories and from the cities where they have been driven by rural unemployment caused by increasing population pressures. Thus a second social class, or more properly a subdivision of the great body of workers, has come into being which tends to be more subject to discontent with its own state than are the peasants, whose tensions are relieved by traditional rural patterns and relationships. The relationship between these workers and their superiors is characterized by the same absence of communication that exists between landlord and tenant, by the failure of the former to supply any positive production incentives, and, in spite of certain paternalistic benefits, by an inadequate wage scale. Moreover, systems of public administration and services have tended to be inadequate to deal with the felt needs of the people and the growing possibilities for development.

These chronic causes of poverty and unrest among both peasants and workers in the Arab states have been aggravated by further pressures resulting from the mass migration of the Palestine refugees, who, in a sense, are an exemplification of the poverty, underemployment, and discontent which permeate the area. Communism is another cause of discontent which has been particularly significant since World War II, when relations between the Near East and the West began to shift so greatly. . . . Among both farming and laboring groups, Communist influence is still small in comparison to that among the intelligentsia.

Because of the factors discussed above, the vast majority of Arabs and Iranians live in a relatively deprived and frustrated state. Despite recent progress, illiteracy runs to at least 70 or 80 per cent in all of the countries under consideration except Lebanon. Annual incomes per family (not per capita) average $200 to $300. Infant mortality is exceedingly high. Chronic diseases like trachoma, bilharzia, hookworm, typhoid, and dysentery sap vitality. Population pressures in Egypt, Lebanon, and Jordan are among the heaviest in the world at a time when agricultural production per capita, although growing, remains very low. In the whole of the Arab world the total area under cultivation is about the same as that in the state of Iowa. In the Near Eastern countries one third to one acre of land per capita is under cultivation. A small percentage of the population owns a large percentage of the land; in one country, 0.2 per cent owns more than half. Almost three quarters of the farm population owns no land, or owns plots that are too small to pay for themselves. Housing and sanitary conditions are for the most part deplorable.

Signs of Social Discontent

Let us examine the effect that this traditional lot has exercised in recent years on the farmers and workers, on the one hand, and on the government leaders on the other. The peasants are clearly more restless than they were. It has been said that, partly because of the impact of Communist propaganda, the peasants in many countries are being converted from a state of passive misery to one of alert and active misery. . . .

Evidences of restlessness also have increased in the industrial labor field in recent years. Two striking differences, however, are the much greater degree of organization of the industrial workers as compared with farm workers and the greater influence of communism among the former. Strikes greatly outnumber peasant riots, and their announced aims are much more varied. . . .

Remedies

There is little doubt that a broad and tangible effort has been made to meet the challenge which social discontent presents. Some of the responsibility has, of course, been assumed by private individuals. On the agricultural side, an outstanding example is Hussayn Ibish, who in the last four years has turned the title of lands in his villages south of Damascus over to the farmers who work the land. In Lebanon a group of financiers has raised a significant amount of capital for a "100-village plan" under which they hope to stimulate farm improvement and higher rural living standards by means of private loans. As to private efforts in the labor field, it is perfectly possible to find private plants in the Near East with modern attitudes as well as modern machinery. Factory clinics, cafeterias, playgrounds, vacations with pay, and other mutual benefits to labor and industry that took long years to develop in our own country are making their appearance under private initiative in the Near East, even if the pace is not so rapid as could be desired.

As for the government response to the challenge, perhaps the clearest indicators of intent are the national budgets. Generally speaking, expenditures for items relating to social and economic development have increased not only on an absolute basis for the past several years but also, and perhaps more significantly, on a basis of percentage of total expenditures. From 20 to 40 per cent of Arab and Iranian budget expenditures appears under ministries of agriculture, social affairs, education, public health, national economy, labor, communications, and public works. In most of the budgets the percentage for this type of expenditure is higher than that for defense purposes. In several of the countries separate development or production budgets have recently made their appearance again, reflecting in a general way the awakening of the legislatures and governments to the need for improving the economy and the standards of living. In Iraq 70 per cent of the country's revenues from oil company operations is by law devoted to development purposes. In Iran present legislation requires that all oil revenues be used for economic development.

The degree to which these expenditures directly benefit the peasant and working classes naturally varies and in most cases could probably be considerably increased. The amounts involved, however, are much higher than ever before and are a tangible demonstration that a new concept is gaining ground in the Near East, namely, the idea that progress can be made through programs of general economic improvement based on raising the living standards of farmers and industrial workers.

Land Tenure Legislation

Near Eastern governments probably have introduced more legislation and decrees pertaining to land during the last five years than during the preceding several decades. Moreover, the objectives have been greatly broadened so as to fit in with over-all development, in addition to benefiting individual peasants by providing improved tenancy rights or eventual outright ownership, liberal credit, better marketing conditions, and technical guidance.

Among the particularly noteworthy legislation is the Shah of Iran's decree of 1951 turning a quarter of a million acres of royal lands over to peasants on liberal credit terms. Another is

Iraq's "Law for the Development and Cultivation of the Dujaila Lands," passed in 1946 and subsequently expanded, under which Dujaila and five other projects for the settlement of landless peasants have been put into effect, with six more in preparation. A million acres of state lands are being prepared for future distribution to landless peasants with an opportunity for eventual ownership.

Other similar measures include Syria's Decree No. 96 regarding the distribution of state lands to peasants; Egypt's law of 1939 for the establishment of rural social centers . . . and Egypt's land reform law of 1952—one of the earliest laws instituted by the present regime. The latter limits individual ownership to 200 feddans (207 acres), provides for compensation to landowners and distribution of the excess among peasants, and guards against further fragmentation of plots under five feddans. To these measures might be added numerous agreements for technical assistance in the field of land tenure with the United States (private foundations as well as the Government), the United Kingdom, and United Nations agencies, particularly the Food and Agriculture Organization, and UNESCO.

In Iran both the United States Foreign Operations Administration [FOA] and private foundations have used the Shah's land-distribution program as a basis for other development projects. They have provided technical assistance to the twelve villages which were first distributed under the Shah's program and have demonstrated how, through a system of community development, supervised credit and technical aid can create independent farmers out of poverty-stricken peasants. To date over 5,000 farmers have received lands under the land distribution program, and a bank initiated with FOA help is serving the needs of the more than 50,000 families in Crown Land villages.

The degree to which these and related laws and project agreements have been implemented has varied considerably. All of them encounter technical, financial, psychological, and political obstacles in the search for an improved substitute for the old system. Nevertheless, they reflect an unprecedented effort on the part of current Near Eastern leaders to give the mass of peasants better leases on their lands and on their lives.

Labor Measures

Basic labor legislation is not quite so new or dramatic as are land reform measures in the Near East. The labor codes of Lebanon, Syria, and Iran were enacted in 1946; Iraq's code underwent important revisions that same year; and the Saudi decree for hours, age limits, and disability compensation was issued in 1947.

The interest of the Arab States in the International Labor Organization [ILO] has been a stimulus to measures which meet the challenge of labor unrest. Lebanon, Iraq, Syria, Iran, and Egypt are all members; Egypt holds an assistant director generalship. In addition to participating in ILO projects, several of the states are engaged in technical assistance projects with FOA in such fields as statistics, worker education and vocational training, industrial safety, and arbitration methods. Although improved laws regarding strikes, unionization, and other aspects of labor are clearly needed, generally speaking the greatest need in most Near Eastern countries is for improved implementation of existing legislation, through the ministries of labor or social affairs which have been created recently by several countries.

The one Near Eastern country which has recently introduced rather sweeping labor legislation is Egypt. The Egyptian Trade Union Act of 1942 expressly excluded the unionization of agricultural workers and also prohibited individual workers' unions from joining a single national federation. These situations were reversed by the new government in December 1952, less than six months after it took office. As a result of the new decree, more than sixty groups of agricultural workers have applied for union charters and the establishment of a general confederation of unions is receiving serious study. The latter move might enable Egypt's more responsible and effective labor officials to lead poorly organized unions into effective operation.

Egypt's labor legislation presents one problem which has not been resolved: it prohibits the dismissal of an employee, if he chooses to appeal, without permission from the courts. This provision is of particular concern to foreign investors; it also is a potential financial and administrative burden on all firms, especially those in seasonal manufacturing. The Egyptian government has been described by some observers as prolabor but not antibusiness, and the trend is toward a modification of this legislation. Egypt is gaining experience daily in the field of industrial relations, and it has clearly accepted the challenge of labor unrest and the conditions underlying it.

Major Development Projects

In recent years and months Near Eastern leaders have spent less time pointing to rivers and ports that should be developed and more time looking over plans on which cost estimates can be based, firms hired, and money appropriated or borrowed. . . .

Iran has practically completed plans calling for the expenditure of $700 million for economic development. Although these figures may at first glance appear fantastically high, they are actually well within Iran's financial ability, based on its potential oil income. This income will reach $180 million annually by the end of 1957, and, as stated above, Iranian legislation requires that all of it be devoted to economic development.

The Lebanese government has just invited selected firms to bid on the engineering plans and supervisory contract for the first phase of the Litani River Basin project; preparatory work for this phase was done by a twenty-four-man team financed by FOA. Well over $100 million is contemplated as the eventual expenditure on this self-liquidating power and irrigation project.

Some of the world's greatest engineers have recently pronounced Egypt's High Aswan Dam project feasible. Expenditures over the next decade may exceed half a billion dollars for the largest dam and reservoir in the world. The project, as conceived, would increase Egypt's acreage by at least one fourth and probably more. UNRWA [United Nations Relief Works Agency for Palestine refugees in the Near East] engineers have recently completed a study under which sweet water from the Nile will be siphoned under the Suez Canal and used to irrigate Sinai lands which can support more than 50,000 refugees. The Unified Plan for the Development of the Jordan Valley is not yet adopted and still faces important obstacles. The value of crop production in the valley could conceivably increase tenfold in less than a decade if all goes well.

Syria is developing the port of Latakia with its own finances and is well advanced in the engineering of its Ghab Swamp irrigation and drainage projects, among others. Iraq's Wadi Tharthar flood control project on the Tigris is expected to be completed next year. Other important development projects in the Near East include the improvement of transportation and communication between urban and rural districts and the construction of research laboratories and extension stations.

Development boards have been established in recent years in Iraq, Jordan, Lebanon, and Egypt, and one has been in existence in Iran for years. In several of these countries, the boards are considering investment and development surveys made by the International Bank for Reconstruction and Development (IBRD). Iran has received substantial United States economic aid for several years, and in Egypt, Jordan, and Lebanon, United States economic aid programs over and above technical assistance have been inaugurated in the last few months with a United States contribution of $59 million. Those who dismissed such projects as unrealizable dreams ten years ago must now take account not only of the tremendously augmented oil revenues, the availability of United States and IBRD funds, and the increased file of completed blueprints, but also the desire of the Near Eastern leaders to avail themselves of these new factors as a means of reducing the unrest and attaining stability. Granted that it is only a beginning, it is an answer to a challenge. It is significant that a new word is on the tongues of Near Eastern engineers and officials—"scheduling"—that is, the synchronization of many phases of land reclamation, resettlement, and other projects toward the proper culmination of the program.

Other Programs

Although the major development projects involve external financial planning assistance, the recent growth of international cooperation as a means of improving the welfare of peasant and

worker is more widely revealed in the field of technical assistance. Well over a million dollars a year is being spent in the
Arab countries and Iran by the United Nations specialized agencies for regional meetings and for individual advisory projects in
fields covered by the World Health Organization, the International Labor Organization, the Food and Agriculture Organization, and UNESCO. The economic studies and recommendations
made in Syria and Iraq by IBRD paid considerable attention to
the social aspects of agriculture and industry, and this is likely
to be the case in the bank's forthcoming survey of Jordan.
United States technical assistance programs, now in their fifth
year, will involve United States expenditures in excess of $22
million in the current fiscal year in five Arab countries and Iran.
While the proportion of projects with direct and early benefits
to peasants and workers is difficult to calculate precisely, many
of the projects testify to the growing cooperation between Near
Eastern leaders and international and foreign technical assistance
organizations in the interests of resource development and the
popular welfare.

The desire for improved education and broader opportunities
is hardly new in the Near East. It has been more than a thousand years since Al-Ashar University was founded at Cairo. It
was almost twenty years ago that the government of Iraq offered
teaching positions to every member of the graduating class of
the College of Arts and Sciences at the American University of
Beirut—at starting salaries higher than in most other professions.
The last decade, however, has brought the broadest and most
concerted effort, coincident with the attainment of political independence of most of the countries under discussion. In Lebanon, for example, 100 government primary schools were established in the 21 years between World Wars I and II, whereas
more than 700 such schools have been established since the end
of World War II. Moreover, action on the need for vocational
training has increased greatly, as is shown particularly by the
numerous requests for technical assistance in this field.

Near Eastern governments have also taken steps toward the
establishment of public-health and public-administration practices
which will be of tangible benefit to the people as a whole. Sur-

face evidence of this is to be found in recent regional conferences on both topics held at Beirut; in the enrollment of students from throughout the area in the public-health and public-administration schools established at the American University of Beirut in 1951; in the percentage of the more than 2,000 Iranian and Arab students now in the United States who are studying public health and administration; and in the numerous demonstration projects and special studies under technical assistance programs in these fields. The new emphasis on environmental sanitation measures such as drainage and malaria control, as well as the clinical work in rural social centers, reflect the grassroots approach. How effective it has been to date is a less important question than how effective it will be after a little more time has elapsed and the infinite problems of training and tradition have been more fully dealt with.

Sum Total of Response

We have considered the problem of social discontent among the peasant working classes of the Near East and its causes, as well as examples of its recent manifestation. In conclusion one must ask whether the sum total of the public response to the challenge of social discontent is effective.

Obviously such discontent long since stimulated the assumption of responsibility by some Near Eastern leaders, but the need is now recognized by increasing numbers. Although the extent to which the causes of unrest have been reduced is open to question, certainly effective approaches to a solution of these causes now occupy the thoughts and energies of a significant number of the area's leaders. In my opinion they have walked a rough and circuitous path, but they have come upon the right road. The distance behind them on that road must be measured in rods while the distance ahead is a matter of miles. The important thing, however, is that they are on it in force and with growing energy to finish the race. I am glad that there are Western way stations, both private and public, where the helping hands of free men will be extended to help them.

Much remains to be done to meet the needs of the people of the Near East, but already great and encouraging steps have been taken. A new wind is blowing, and if, as a result of progressive measures by their own countrymen, the average peasant and worker can continue to find new hope, it seems certain that they will not turn to the Kremlin for a solution to their problems.

CONFLICTS WITHIN THE ARAB LEAGUE [2]

The unifying forces in the Arab world stem almost entirely from tradition and history, ideas and aspirations, and, first and foremost, from language and civilization. There is little ethnic homogeneity between the various parts of the Arab world; the direct descendants of the ethnically Arab conquerors cannot be supposed to form a substantial percentage of the populations of today's Arab countries. It is the Arabic language and civilization that made these countries and their peoples "Arab" and that form the main basis for the aspirations for Arab unity.

Islamic beliefs and traditions and the all-permeating rhythm of Islamic practices form the second major force for unity. That force, to be sure, has been modified and weakened by the influx of pre-Islamic local beliefs, superstitions and practices and by the sectarian splits in Islam . . . ; it has also been weakened by the decline of the influence of religious beliefs and practices on growing strata of urban intelligentsia and modernist leadership. Moreover, it does not apply to the non-Moslem elements in the Arab world—the majority of the population of the Lebanon, and sizable non-Moslem minorities in most of the Arab countries. The Islamic aspect of Arab unity, on the other hand, introduces an extraneous force of solidarity with non-Arab Moslem nations and countries on a pan-Islamic basis. Nevertheless, it cannot be gainsaid that Islamic traditions, beliefs and practices form one of the most potent elements of Arab unity.

The traditions and memories of a united Arab empire, interwoven with Islamic traditions and strengthened by the more

[2] From "Ten Years of the Arab League," by J. S. Raleigh, writer on the Middle East. *Middle Eastern Affairs*. 6:65-77. March 1955. Reprinted by permission.

recent memories of being united under the Ottoman Empire (not really an "Arab" unity, but political unity nevertheless) form the third major force working for Arab unity. This unity of the past was not a monolithic unity embracing all the Arab countries; North Africa seldom, and only for short periods, belonged to it; Egypt and the Arabian Peninsula have gone their own ways for centuries—*de facto* if not *de jure*. Memories of unity are therefore strongest among the countries of the "Fertile Crescent" (Iraq, Syria, Lebanon, Jordan, and until 1948, Palestine). It is the intangible feeling of belonging together, the consciousness of Arabism, into which those traditions and memories crystallize, over and above the objective categories of language and civilization, religion and custom, that is today the major force for Arab unity.

Contemporary needs and considerations for regional unity or cooperation in the fields of economics and development, communications and river control, health and pest control, etc. should not be listed here, since they do not in themselves make for *Arab* unity, but should, logically, make for *regional* cooperation (including the non-Arab states of the region). However, grafted as they are on the traditional, cultural and emotional trends towards Arab unity, they may well be considered an additional force for unity.

Against these forces for unity are pitted strong trends of separatism and parochialism. Separate national entities have developed over the centuries, in spite of the unifying forces of language and religion. Different dialects; different local customs, which to some extent developed in the millennia before the Arab conquest; different physical environments and therefore different economic needs and developments; different historical developments and therefore different traditions and memories—all these make the idea of Arab unity an abstract concept, remote from all the needs and realities of daily life.

There is hardly an Arab leader who would not pay ample and flowery lip service to the idea of Arab unity, but in actuality separate loyalties have grown stronger than the concept of Arab unity. Nationalism entrenched itself more and more firmly whenever and wherever separate entities achieved political independence, while pan-Arab ideas and aspirations were vigorously proclaimed by those national movements which were still fighting for independence. . . . This development of separate nationalism is mainly a growth of the period between the two World Wars, and its history is inseparably linked with the Hashemite dynasty (King Hussein of Hijaz and his sons Feisal and Abdullah and their descendants) on the one hand, and the policies and activities of Great Britain and France on the other.

During the nineteen-twenties and 'thirties the idea of Arab unity was relegated to occasional conventions, speeches and resolutions. It could not be real politics since two of the Arab states, Syria and Lebanon, were not even nominally independent; the others were fighting to transform their nominal independence into real independence; Egypt, the strongest, most populous and politically most experienced Arab state, stood aloof; and inter-Arab dynastic rivalries were still at the boiling point (the Hashemite princes had not yet acquiesced in Ibn Saud's conquest of their ancestral domain, Hijaz; trouble was constant on the Saudi-Iraqi and Saudi-Jordanian borders; Saudi Arabia and Yemen were even engaged in a full-fledged war in 1934).

It was Great Britain who took the initiative in solving the problems and overcoming the obstacles to Arab unity and it was, incidentally, the Palestine problem that served as the catalytic agent to bring the Arab states together for the first time. . . .

When the British felt, in the early forties, that the time was ripe to give the idea of Arab unity concrete form, it was apparent to them that a full-fledged federation or confederacy was out of the question: social, economic and political heterogeneity were too marked, separate national independence too firmly entrenched, mutual confidence too feeble. The question was whether to be content with a loose alliance of the independent Arab states, or to begin with a more complete union in a geographically restricted area where Arab unity was more alive and realistically more possible. Such an area was the "Fertile Crescent."

Egypt had been a separate entity for many decades, even centuries; the Arabian Peninsula was a remote desert; but the separate states of the Fertile Crescent were relatively recent creations. Their boundaries had not yet become fully rooted in tradition; those boundaries had, moreover, been imposed and demarcated, in 1918-1920, without much consultation with the populations concerned, and even against their wishes. The Hashemite dynasty which ruled in Iraq and Jordan regarded the rest of the Fertile Crescent—Syria, the Lebanon and Palestine— as rightfully its domain; it was only because of British betrayal of promises, Arab-French clashes and Anglo-French differences in 1918-1919 that Feisal had been forced out of Damascus.

Logically, the "Greater Syria" scheme (calling for union of Syria—with or without the Lebanon—with Jordan, and originally with Palestine as well) and the Fertile Crescent scheme (advocating the same union, but with the addition of Iraq) need not have been "Hashemite" schemes. It is theoretically possible to advocate union of Syria with her neighbors, under *Syrian* leadership and a republican regime, instead of under a Hashemite monarchy. In reality, both schemes have been closely and almost exclusively associated with the Hashemite dynasty (with an undercurrent of rivalry and jealousy between the two branches of the dynasty itself as to which one was to be dominant) and opposed by all the foes of that dynasty.

Again, logically and theoretically, a close union or federation of the Fertile Crescent countries, and a loose alliance of that federation with all the other Arab states, need not be mutually incompatible, and the protagonists of Greater Syria were quite right when they maintained just that. Indeed, most plans broached or submitted for the union of Syria and Iraq and/or Jordan took care to present that union as only the nucleus or first link of a wider alliance with the other Arab states. In the context of inter-Arab relations and realities, however, a Fertile Crescent or Greater Syria unity and an all-embracing Arab alliance or league are mutually incompatible. Both Saudi Arabia and Egypt are strongly and unalterably opposed to any territorial aggrandizement on the part of the Hashemites, to any increase in their prestige, power and inter-Arab position, in fact, to any change in the territorial and political status quo in the Arab world, and their cooperation and participation in an all-Arab league has always been conditional on the jealous preservation of that status quo.

It was natural that an upsurge of Hashemite plans for unity and expansion should take place in the later years of the second World War. French power in the Levant—the major obstacle to any Greater Syria scheme—was waning; British ties and sympathies with the Hashemite dynasty had become even stronger as a result of Abdullah's unflinching loyalty and the Iraqi events of 1941 which showed that it was only the Hashemite house and its political supporters that could keep Iraq on the British side; in power in Egypt was a Wafd cabinet which was rumored to be less hostile to the Hashemite dynasty and its plans than were King Farouk and the other parties; the British were in over-all operative, military and political control of the Middle East.

Arab unity plans crystallized in 1942, in the famous Blue Book presented by the veteran pro-Hashemite Iraqi statesman, Nuri as-Said, which suggested a Greater Syria state (with local autonomy for the Jews of Palestine and the Christians of Lebanon), federated with Iraq, and an alliance between that Fertile Crescent federation and the other Arab states. The scheme failed, as it was bound to, to attract Egyptian and Saudi sympathy, and during 1943 it became clear that an Arab league could only be based on the inter-Arab status quo. The Arab League, established in March 1945 under Egyptian leadership, is therefore—paradoxical as it may sound—not a pan-Arab achievement but, on the contrary, a bulwark designed to protect the separate national independence of the Arab states, the inter-Arab status quo, against pan-Arab union schemes. True, the Hashemites and their supporters did not renounce their plans and ambitions, and implementation of their schemes would be legal in terms of the charter of the Arab League. Constitutionally, therefore, the Arab League is based on an essential controversy that has not been solved; in fact, it was only by leaving that decisive question open and ambiguous that the foundation of the League, cooperation between Egypt and Saudi Arabia on the one hand, and the Hashemite states on the other, was possible at all. [The original League consisted of Egypt, Iraq, Jordan, Saudi Arabia, Syria, Lebanon, and Yemen. Libya was admitted in 1953.—Ed.]. . .

The character of the Arab League as a loose alliance of sovereign states, with no power of its own and committed to the preservation of the inter-Arab status quo, finds full expression in the League charter. Its main operative provision, Article 7, lays down that no decision taken by the League shall be considered in force unless and until ratified by the member-states, and that, moreover, no state shall be bound by any decision for which it has not itself voted. In cases of aggression, there is no provision for automatic assistance; all that is called for is consultation (Article 6), there is no commitment whatsoever on the part of the member-states. Provision is made for the deposit of treaties concluded by the member-states with the League secretariat, but no provision for prior consultation, and no limitation is set on such treaties (Article 17). At the same time, the essential question of pan-Arab schemes was constitutionally left open: member-states that desired "closer cooperation and stronger links than provided for in this Charter" were free to conclude between themselves any treaty that they wished (Article 9).

The weakness and looseness of the alliance were obvious, and attempts to tighten the links between the sovereign member-states, to strengthen the commitments made to the League and increase the power of the supranational body have been continuous. Plans for a tighter federation were submitted from time to time, both by pro-Hashemite statesmen with an eye on Greater Syria, and by anti-Hashemite circles desirous of strengthening the Egyptian-led guardian of the status quo, but they always were buried in committees. Only one decision of the League—connected with the Palestine question and unconstitutional in legal terms of the Charter—went beyond the original loose Charter. In the spring of 1950 a decision was unanimously adopted that any member-state which concluded a separate peace with Israel should be automatically expelled from the League.

Otherwise, the only advance towards a tightening of the Arab alliance was the Arab Collective Security Pact, signed in April 1950 and in force since August 1952. That pact again leaves open, legally and constitutionally, the essential question of Greater Syria. Apart from its fundamental anti-Israeli contents, it was conceived as an Egyptian move to forestall any Iraqi-Hashemite schemes for union and aggrandizement. That much was openly stated. It serves in that sense only if it is assumed that the mere strengthening of an all-Arab alliance based on the status quo would by itself prevent the implementation of any Hashemite schemes, for the pact itself does not contain any reference to the problem. The basic questions are again left open: Is it possible to put teeth into an alliance whose members are not prepared to delegate to it any power, any sovereignty? Does the strengthening of an alliance based on the status quo *per se* prevent members of the alliance from attempting to change the status quo in their own favor?

In legal-constitutional terms, the security pact goes beyond the League's charter on three points: (a) it provides for military cooperation and for a definite mutual defense commitment (Article 2) and establishes machinery for such cooperation; (b) it limits the freedom of the member-states to conclude treaties to such agreements as would not conflict with the letter and spirit of the Pact (Article 10); and (c) Article 6 stipulates the decisions of the defense council adopted by a two-thirds majority shall be binding on all the members (differing from the League charter in that it also applies to those who opposed such decisions). It is on those additions to the original loose alliance of the League charter that inter-Arab politics have hinged for the last two or three years.

Is Iraq, therefore, free to conclude a defense agreement with Turkey and the West (as Iraq mantains), or would such an agreement be contradictory to the letter and spirit of the collective security pact (as Egypt charges)? The binding character of the defense council's decisions has been subject to formal reservations on the part of Iraq and Yemen, and these in turn raise serious doubts about their validity.

The impact of the Arab League on Arab and Middle Eastern policies and situations should be gauged under three headings: the degree of practical cooperation achieved among the member-states; the creation of a united front in foreign politics and of a "bloc" in world affairs; the extent to which the League has been able to prevent, modify or arbitrate inter-Arab disputes and rivalries.

A detailed account of the League's successes and failures in practical cooperation would go beyond the scope of this article. Let it be said, however, that in this field the successes have been few, the failures many, and that the League is still submerged in unending planning, blueprinting, debating and drafting. In the sphere of military cooperation, real coordination was lacking in the one trial-in-the-field, the Palestine war of 1948. In spite of some progress since then not very much has been created beyond the pact itself; there is no unified command or staff, and hardly any coordination of equipment and training. . . .

Cooperation in the judicial field, including an ambitious project for an inter-Arab high court of justice, has been planned and mapped out for years, but the only thing that has come of any of the projects are several extradition agreements which do not embrace all the Arab states and which are, in fact, bilateral agreements common between countries all over the world. Ambitious projects for an all-Arab citizenship and passport have not yet come to fruition; even a plan to grant special all-Arab passports to Palestinian refugees has not yet fully materialized. Special mutual privileges, such as the elimination of visas, have been bilaterally granted in some cases—but then, there was no need for a pan-Arab movement to achieve a degree of cooperation that is usual among friendly states.

The sphere of economic cooperation, too, has been marked by plans, schemes and blueprints rather than by achievements. . . .

Neither have large-scale inter-Arab schemes for economic cooperation and joint development yielded any practical results. . . .

There is a considerable amount of cultural and educational cooperation—mainly an exchange of teachers (mostly Egyptian, and to a degree Palestinian, being sent to such Arab states as Kuwait, Libya, etc. which suffer from a lack of educational personnel), and students (the training of non-Egyptian students in Egypt), as well as textbooks and books in general. It is doubtful, however, whether it is really the Arab League that is responsible for this cultural exchange. . . .

While the Saudi-Yemeni war of 1934 was the last inter-Arab armed conflict, it can hardly be maintained that the existence of the Arab League has mitigated or diminished inter-Arab rivalry, conflict and tension. The area of greater inter-Arab unity of purpose undoubtedly is the common hatred of Israel, and the greatest display of that unity was the Arab League's war against Israel in 1948. And yet that same war brought to the fore intrinsic conflicts and tensions that even comradeship-in-arms could not overcome. The original decision not to wage the war with the regular Arab armies, but only to maintain and equip volunteer forces, was changed, mainly by Egypt, primarily to prevent King Abdullah [of Jordan] from taking over the Arab half of Palestine and then making his own separate arrangements with Israel. A unified supreme command, with Abdullah at its head, was solemnly set up, but it never had a chance to function; each one of the five invading armies marched separately and fought separately. Conflict between Jordan and Egypt over the control of the Hebron-Bethlehem area flared up in actual armed clashes. . . . The campaign of public mutual recriminations, especially between Jordan and Egypt, that followed these developments sounded like psychological warfare between bitter enemies.

In the spring of 1950 the League appeared to be on the brink of dissolution; Egypt, Syria and Saudi Arabia were bent on expelling Jordan for having annexed the Arab half of Palestine, and King Abdullah was so adamant in his resolve to consummate that annexation that he refused to consent even to the face-saving formula, devised by Iraq and Lebanon, as mediators, that the annexation was "temporary" and that Abdullah was holding Arab Palestine "in trust" for the League until the day of the final reckoning with Israel and the "solution of the Palestine problem." Surface unity was preserved only by recourse, again, to the unifying factor of anti-Israel policies: Abdullah abandoned the idea of a separate peace with Israel, bowing to the League, and agreed to a League decision outlawing and denouncing any such separate negotiations.

The Greater Syria idea and the Fertile Crescent scheme have caused ever-recurring crises and tensions, particularly whenever Syria herself was weak and wide open to Iraqi intervention and propaganda (and Egyptian and Saudi counter-intervention and counter-propaganda). In the summer of 1949, relations became so strained that both Iraq and Syria dispatched troops to their frontiers; armed clashes were prevented only by the threat of Egyptian intervention. Mutual recriminations and accusations on the dispatch of undercover agents, interference in Syrian affairs, participation in Syria's coups d'état, the expenditure of large amounts of money to "buy" politicians, newspapers, parties and army officers have for years resounded throughout the Arab world.

The latest crisis over Iraq's conclusion of a separate defense alliance with Turkey [later broadened into the Baghdad Pact— Ed.]; the furious attempts of Egypt and Saudi Arabia to prevent consummation of that alliance; Egypt's threat to leave the League or at least the Collective Security Pact, or to have Iraq expelled from both; the hostile propaganda campaign, especially that emanating from Radio Cairo and its "Voice of the Arabs"—are too fresh in the memory of all observers of the Middle Eastern scene to need recounting.

It would seem, after the first ten years of its existence, that the Arab League has neither succeeded in coordinating inter-Arab policies, mitigating or eliminating inter-Arab tensions, or solving inter-Arab problems. In spite of mediation attempts by individual member-states, especially the Lebanon, the League's Council has served as a sounding board for recriminations rather than as a force for unity and conciliation.

Loose alliance of sovereign states that the League is, based on the status quo of its separate members, its main contribution to the political stature of those states is in the presentation to the outside world of a united political bloc. This united front is strongest, most visible and psychologically firmest in the Arab struggle against Israel. Other instances in which such an all-Arab united front was maintained were in the Arab campaign against France in the Syrian crisis of 1945, in permanent anti-French agitation over Tunisia and Morocco, and in a consistent anticolonial attitude. These attributes of Arab policies also form the basis for Arab cooperation in the so-called Asian-African bloc. The same united Arab front wishes, however, to establish itself on all other political fronts, too—in Arab dealings with the West, in world politics, in the United Nations.

This attempt to create a united front has by no means been completely successful. For several years now the Arab position and Arab votes in the United Nations, for instance, have usually been split, Iraq and Lebanon taking a pro-Western attitude and voting with the West; Egypt, Syria, Saudi Arabia and Yemen in most cases taking a neutralist attitude. Whether this neutralism is basic and permanent, as some observers believe, or whether, as others maintain, it is a tactical device designed to obtain more benefits from the West, and whether Iraq's pro-Western outlook is sincere or also primarily a tactical move—this split between pro-Western Iraqi (and Lebanese) policies and Egyptian-Saudi neutralism has now finally come to a head in the heated inter-Arab controversy over the Iraqi-Turkish pact.

Although thus split on the most decisive issues of contemporary world politics, the League's façade of a united external front is nevertheless being rigidly maintained. In the highly emotional climate of Middle Eastern public opinion, the anti-Israel, North African, anticolonial aspects of Arab policies may well be sufficient to maintain that front. The hope that, in spite of Iraq's separate treaty, some deal can still be made with the West which would be based on the League as a whole and its collective security pact, is studiously maintained and nurtured (by some Western statesmen and by Pakistan as well as by Arab leaders). . . .

A rigid federation, a true union, a consistent united front might well have broken down under the continuing stresses and strains of inter-Arab dissension and dispute. The very looseness of the Arab League, the very noncommittal character of most of its instruments, now become an asset instead of a liability. So loose an alliance, so non-binding an instrument may well survive even those crises, even that lack of effective action, even that absence of ultimate confidence, that have characterized inter-Arab relations and the League of Arab States during the first ten years of its existence.

EGYPT'S ASWAN DAM PROJECT [3]

By [the Egyptian] President Nasser's bold nationalization of the Suez Canal on July 26, 1956, Egypt estimated that she could afford to carry alone the burden of financing the great High Dam project on the Nile.

This would be assuming, of course, that the revolutionary regime in Egypt gets away with the dramatic and somewhat vengeful seizure of the foreign-operated East-West waterway and all of its assets.

If the current annual income of the Suez Canal, estimated . . . at about 35 million Egyptian pounds, or about $100 million, were to be diverted entirely to Colonel Nasser's vast dream of harnessing the Nile, experts believe Egypt could just manage to scrape through without too much damage to her economy.

These estimates must, however, remain on a purely hypothetical basis. What would happen to the present high standard of maintenance on this vital international shipping lane would be a matter of serious concern.

It was obvious, indeed virtually admitted, that President Nasser had expropriated the Suez Canal Company to prove to the world that Egypt could get around the somewhat crushing withdrawal by the United States and Britain of offers to help finance the High Dam at Aswan. . . .

A projection into Egypt's economic future combined with her own almost daily announcement of new plans for other industrialization projects, clearly indicated that Egypt would have slipped into a deficit economy even with foreign loans and grants for the High Dam.

It is not that Egypt's economy is not sound today. But it is Egypt's ability to control her ambitious industrialization dreams and maintain a stable government through the long period of austerity that has created doubts in London and Washington.

Egypt's economy is and will be for some time based almost entirely on agriculture, with cotton as the main crop. . . .

[3] From "Nasser's Bold Plans Link Canal and Dam," by Osgood Caruthers, New York *Times* correspondent in Egypt. New York *Times*. p E5. July 29, 1956. Reprinted by permission.

Since the negotiations began between the Western powers and Egypt on financial aid for the High Dam, it . . . has become more and more difficult to estimate how much of Egypt's future production was being committed to trade with the Soviet bloc not only for arms but also for capital goods.

To the coldly calculating eye of the economist it was not the political implication of this shift to the progressively increasing trade with the East that mattered. It was the question of how far Egypt could afford to plunge into an expensive industrialization program that had peculiarly Marxist overtones.

The conclusion was that Egypt could not afford such a program without making continual demands on the donor countries to keep her solvent while the High Dam was under construction. Although Egypt has a relatively sound economy, she has one of the lowest standards of living in the world. To force added austerity upon her people under such circumstances would be harsh action from the humanistic point of view and could possibly become politically dangerous. . . .

The estimate of the annual amount Egypt would have had to spend on the High Dam . . . was made on the basis of the original plan, in which Egypt would have provided $900 million of her own money and the Western powers and the World Bank would have offered the $400 million remainder. [The cost of the project was estimated at $1.3 billion.—Ed.]

If Egypt goes ahead with President Nasser's avowed plan to build the High Dam alone the average annual expenditure on the project will run up to 30 million pounds over the fifteen-year [construction] period, which would create a deficit . . . [even] disregarding all additional industrialization projects the revolutionary regime hopes to undertake.

Nevertheless, economists estimate that if Egypt can realize at least the better part of the new annual revenue of 35 million pounds from the expropriated Suez Canal and can curb her appetite for other ambitious short-range projects, the great High Dam could be built.

It is the belief of most economic observers that this was what President Nasser's economic experts had in mind when they advised him that seizure of the Suez Canal would not only be a bold political move, but also would make his greatest dream possible.

[For an account of developments following the seizure of the Canal, see the concluding articles in Section I—Ed.]

THE PROSPECT OF MORE WATER [4]

A disenchanting moment for a tourist . . . occurs when he stands on the banks of the Jordan. Having abetted an illusion that this stream is at least as majestic as the Delaware at Callicoon or the Connecticut at Brattleboro, he is dismayed to find the creek no larger than the Bronx River, running dishwater-hued in a trench between bare mountains. . . . [Yet] outright war over control of this creek remains a depressing possibility. . . . Israel maintains a sovereign right to divert Jordan water at any moment. Syria swears she will start shooting the instant the Israelis begin digging.

The point of extreme tension is the Jisr Banat Yaacob (bridge of the Daughters of Jacob) south of Lake Huleh, where the Israelis threaten to resume work on an eight-mile diversionary canal. This would be the first link of a chain of canals, tunnels and pipelines designed to carry Jordan waters through the hills of Galilee across the coastal plain and down to the Negev region, which Israel must devlop for her swelling population.

For the first mile or so the diversion canal would be run within the demilitarized zone along the Syrian frontier. This stretch is now commanded by Syrian gun positions.

In October 1953, Syrian protests to the United Nations impelled the Israelis to cease work at Banat Yaacob. The Syrians cited an armistice stipulation that no alterations in the demilitarized zone could take place that would damage existing property rights or give either side a military advantage. Major General Vagn Bennike of Denmark, the then head of the United Nations Truce Supervisory Organization, ordered the project

[4] From "Waters of the Jordan: Key Issue in Mideast," by Homer Bigart, New York *Times* correspondent in Israel. New York *Times*. p E4. May 6, 1956. Reprinted by permission.

halted. His ruling was upheld by the United Nations Security Council "pending urgent examination of the question."

Two and one-half years have elapsed since the Security Council motion, and the Israelis maintain that this is long enough for "urgent examination." But when David Ben-Gurion, Israeli Premier, in talks with Mr. Hammarskjold, insisted Israel was now free to resume the project, the United Nations Secretary General cautioned that the Security Council motion was still in effect.

Is the Jordan River worth fighting over? A lot of Israelis and Arabs apparently think so.

The stark fact is that both Israel and the Hashemite Kingdom of Jordan must soon find a way to share the limited water resources of the Jordan Valley. Pressure of population on both sides—four persons per acre of cultivated land, or twelve times that of the United States—gives terrible urgency to the need for agricultural expansion.

For Israel, tapping the Jordan offers the only possible means of bringing the southern plain into full production and relieving the present heavy dependence on food imports. The water shortage will become desperately acute by 1959, when all underground resources and the Yarkon River, the only perennial stream of any consequence except the Jordan, will have been fully utilized.

Israel's water crisis must be seen against the background of the nation's frustrating climatic and topographical features. Only the northern and central sectors have adequate winter rainfall. In these areas rain occurs only during five months of the year, from November to April. The long summer is hot and dry. In the mountainous northern sector, there is a slight surplus of water because the amount of cultivable land is limited. But in the south potentially fertile lands lie idle without sufficient water to irrigate this semi-desert region.

So long-range water plans must include utilization of the Jordan if Israel is to continue to accept immigrants and hold her food imports below the current level of $65 million a year. . . .

To be reasonably self-sufficient, Israel must expand her ir-rigated area by at least a half million acres in the next ten years, according to government economists.

Israel's northern neighbors, Syria and Lebanon, are compara-tively rich in water resources. But Jordan is desperate.

She has had to absorb a half million Palestinian Arabs and the amount of her cultivated land is not even enough to support the kingdom's own population of 1 million. Even by full utilization of the Yarmuk River (a major tributary of the Jordan running between Jordan and Syria) and of her share of the Jordan River waters, the Kingdom of Jordan would still lack sufficient irrigable land for her present swollen population.

Syria, while largely arid, is under no serious pressure for large-scale water development. Consequently, her opposition to Israel's Jordan water plan strikes observers here as that of a dog in the manger.

Lebanon is relatively self-sufficient. Moreover, she has begun to develop the Litani River, which runs within seven miles of Israel's border. The Israelis still hope Lebanon some day will permit diversion of part of the Litani flow through a tunnel to the Jordan River. Power would be generated on the Israeli side and given to Lebanon in exchange for the Litani water. This project must await the distant day of peaceful Arab-Israeli relations.

The vital importance of Jordan water in the development of a Jewish national home . . . [has long been apparent to Zionists].

[Recently] a plan evolved by Eric Johnston, a special envoy of President Eisenhower, [has been under consideration]. On his fourth mission to the Middle East last year, Mr. Johnston brought a revised plan under which Israel would get 400 million cubic meters of water a year from the Jordan, with Lebanon receiving 35 million cubic meters (from the Hasbani River tribu-tary rising in Lebanon), Syria 132 million cubic meters in three different areas along the Yarmuk and Jordan Rivers and Jordan 477 million cubic meters. Thus three Arab states would receive 62 per cent of the total, with Israel getting 38 per cent.

Israel accepted the Johnston plan "in principle," although she had held out for at least 550 million cubic meters. Israel's reluctance was based partly on the fact that the Johnston plan envisioned control of the program by a United Nations water authority, regarded suspiciously here as an intrusion on sovereignty. Also, the Johnston plan would barely enable Israel to attain an absorptive capacity for a 2 million population.

Yet it was Syria that balked. Although Arab engineers had approved technical details of the plan, the new Syrian government feared it would be forced out of office if it accepted. The Damascus argument was that acceptance of the plan might imply recognition of Israel. Jordan and Lebanon followed Syria's lead.

Confounded by this political frustration, Israel is under dreadful temptation to resume her unilateral water project. She could precipitate a dangerous incident by moving a few bulldozers into the canal site at any moment.

One consideration may hold Israel back. The Jordan project would cost $200 million. Mr. Johnston promised that two-thirds of the amount would be forthcoming from the United States. Israel might risk the loss of American financial support by rashly proceeding at this delicate moment.

ARAB REFUGEES FROM PALESTINE [5]

As of June 1953 there were 872,000 Arab refugees from Palestine registered with the United Nations and residing in Arab countries. These people left their homes in Palestine at the time of the fighting between Israel and the Arab states in 1948. The Arabs say the refugees were driven from their homes by the Israelis. The Israelis say that the refugees left their homes voluntarily in response to the call of the invading Arab armies who assured them that they would soon return in the wake of victorious Arab forces. Disregarding any assessment of blame for what happened, the refugees have not been permitted to return to their homes in what is now Israel and their property has been taken over by the new state.

[5] From "The Arab Refugees and Other Problems in the Near East," a report of the Special Study Mission to the Near East of the House Committee on Foreign Affairs. (House Report no 1250) 83d Congress, 2d session. Superintendent of Documents. Washington 25, D.C. 1954. p3-5, 7.

The United Nations assumed responsibility for providing assistance to the refugees, first, on a purely relief basis and, later, on the basis of relief together with a comprehensive resettlement program. [The financial contribution which the United States has made to this work has been by far the greatest share of the United Nations effort.—Ed.]

Almost no progress [however] has been made in the official United Nations program for resettlement. . . .

The primary reason for the lack of progress in resettlement thus far has been the persistent refusal of Arab leaders to consider any proposal other than that the refugees be allowed to return to their former homes. The suggestion that priority should be given to getting the refugees out of the camps before taking up other questions of Arab-Israel relations has been wholly unacceptable to them. For to have done this, in the Arab view, would have been to renounce all claim to the right of the refugees to return home. Moreover, with public sentiment so aroused over the refugee question, any Arab political leader suggesting an alternative to repatriation in what was formerly Palestine would have been ousted from office and, perhaps, have run the risk of assassination.

A further obstacle to resettlement is the extreme barrenness and poverty of the countries adjacent to Israel in which most of the refugees are located. These are Jordan, Egypt, Lebanon, and Syria. All of these countries are short of water, have large areas of desert, and possess little or no oil. Each has a large proportion of its own population existing at a minimum subsistence level. The only way to provide for large numbers of refugees in these countries is to bring additional land under cultivation. This involves large-scale, high-cost irrigation projects of a complex nature because the sources of water are so limited.

In the judgment of the study mission, however, there are a number of indications that action can and should be initiated immediately which could contribute toward the solution of the refugee problem. One element in the situation is the fact that five years of waiting and resistance have had an effect. Some of the refugees and Arab government officials are beginning to realize that holding out against all United Nations proposals is not certain to result in the ultimate return of the refugees to their homes. . . .

The people not in camps receive United Nations rations but to some extent their integration into the life of the countries where they live has already begun. They have found some sort of shelter and usually some sort of part-time employment. The worst living conditions of refugees observed by the study mission were those of a group of families living in a mosque in Damascus. These people were in the mosque voluntarily in preference to a camp because they preferred to be in the city, with its opportunities for odd jobs and other attractions, than isolated in a camp in the desert. These people are living in misery but they are becoming part of Syria and they are not merely waiting for return to Palestine. When it is recognized that over 50 per cent of these refugees are children under fifteen, few of whom retain any memory of life in Palestine, it can be seen that time is working in the direction of resettlement.

In addition, there is a growing realization that Israel is here to stay. The Arabs know that new settlements have been established all over Israel and that substantial improvements and capital investments have already been made. It is becoming more and more apparent that the return of the Arabs to their homes involves more than the issuance of a decree. Many of the refugees do not want to live under the government of Israel. They feel that they would inevitably be second-class citizens. As people understand that there is no way of going back to life as it was before 1948 they become more receptive to alternatives.

The study mission found that the Arab nations regard the refugee problem as only one element in the larger problem of Israel-Arab relations. . . . The study mission believes that it is futile for the United States to press for a solution of the refugee problem unless the solution is linked to other proposals which will contribute to the alleviation of tensions between the Arab states and Israel.

It is necessary to recognize that among the refugees, particularly those in camps, there is still great hostility to the United

States and to the United Nations. In Lebanon the study mission was permitted to visit only what was acknowledged to be the best refugee camp because the hostility against Americans was so great in the others that the group would not be safe. The United Nations Country Director for Lebanon (a Frenchman) had not visited two of the worst camps for a year because of the hostility of the people toward United Nations officials. Certain refugee leaders, although not living in camps themselves, told the study mission that in some camps the residents would not even allow a window to be repaired since such action would be in the direction of resettlement (because the housing would be made more permanent). Any further steps to be taken with regard to the refugees must give full recognition to these emotional factors.

All of the projects for resettling any substantial number of refugees so far proposed involve large-scale land-reclamation developments, none of which is as yet really under way and all of which will take three or more years to complete. After completion, the process of getting the people in the camps settled on the land and the land into full production will inevitably take several years more. These conditions appear to be unavoidable. The countries in which the refugees are to be settled are among the poorest in terms of agricultural resources to be found in the world, and the refugee farmers have been following a pattern of village life and of farming technique which have not been changed significantly for centuries.

Recommendations

The study mission is convinced that a new approach to solving the refugee problem should be oriented as follows:

First, it is necessary to induce a desire on the part of the Arabs to work out a solution to the problem. Such a desire does not exist at present.

Second, the status of the refugees as a special group of people who are wards of the United Nations should be terminated as soon as possible. The objective should be for refugees to become citizens of the Arab states and, if necessary, they should be made wards of the Arab governments pending their admission to citizenship. This process should not be delayed until new land is available for settlement. Ten years from now the transition will be made more difficult. We do not want the refugees to follow a course comparable to that of the American Indians on reservations.

Third, responsibility for administration of the program should be transferred to the Arab states and should be distributed in such a way as to provide an incentive to the Arab governments to open their doors to the refugees and to assimilate them. . . .

There is [also] no question but that the Arab owners of immovable property which is now being utilized by Israel should receive compensation from Israel. If, because of Israel's limited resources, it is impossible to discharge such obligation for compensation at present, a funding arrangement should be developed so that the rights of the refugees in this respect will not be completely ignored. Prompt action on this problem would go a long way to reduce Arab hostility toward Israel.

The study mission recognizes that its recommendations regarding the refugees are adjusted to current realities, are designed to make a bad situation better, and leave upon the shoulders of the refugees a disproportionate share of the burden. This does not indicate a lack of sympathy with the refugees, however. In the judgment of history, whoever may be blamed for what has happened, it is clearly not the ordinary man from a village in Palestine who was tilling the soil as his ancestors had done before him for more than a thousand years. The hardships which have been imposed upon him and his family are not his fault. He deserves the sympathy and the help of the entire world. In making its recommendations, the study mission believes that the course of action proposed will serve the interests of the refugees better than any alternative which is at present possible. This is a human relations problem and no effort is made here to minimize the seriousness of it.

TURKEY IN TROUBLE [6]

Only yesterday Turkey had seemed a solid rock in the free world's sea of uncertainties. Now it is a bothered bastion. Its economy is sick and its government is flirting with bankruptcy. Its brief but intense experience with democracy is afflicted with a return of the familiar weapons of autocracy.

What has gone wrong, and what can be done about it? These questions, raised for months past, concern more than . . . Premier Adnan Menderes, his government and his 23 million countrymen. All the other allies of NATO have cause to worry about the health of the member that anchors NATO's Eastern wing, provides the allies' largest single bloc of soldiers (the entire Turkish army of 500,000 men), and stands stoutly across the Black Sea from Russia. . . .

The Turkish problem grows in great part out of a commendable urge, an almost feverish yearning, to become overnight a dynamic, industrial nation. For a nation forged only 32 years ago out of the scrap iron of the broken-down Ottoman Empire and the hot will of the late great Kemal Ataturk, for a people who for centuries left the complexities of commerce to their Greek and Armenian subjects, the Turks have made historic progress. In the five years since Premier Menderes left his Opposition bench in the Assembly to lead the Democrats to a stunning upset victory over the Republicans, he has gone all out to expand Turkey's productive capacity.

On the surface, the record has been amazing. Setting aside half its budget for defense, Turkey has put 22 divisions into NATO, doubled its output of steel, cement, textiles. It has built 7,000 miles of road and started a dozen multipurpose dam projects. Its most spectacular gain has been in agriculture, where, with the help of subsidies and 40,000 imported tractors, it has doubled the tilled land and turned the country into an exporter of wheat and cotton.

"But the Turks," explained one important United States official recently, ". . . have tried to cram fifty years' progress into five; they just don't have the economic base to do it." In the midst of great accomplishment, troubles have bred like termites. In the pellmell rush of putting up factories, dredging ports, bulldozing roads, planting new crops, nobody found time or talent to coordinate and manage all the projects. . . .

Pledged to maintain both a free economy and a breakneck pace of expansion, Turkey became more and more overextended. At home, Farmer Menderes staunchly refused . . . to extend the income tax to farmers, who represent 80 per cent of the population and the bulk of Menderes' party's electoral support. The country exhausted its foreign-exchange reserves and ran up foreign debts. . . .

Shortages have grown worse. Chrome-mining firms cannot even get enough foreign exchange to buy dynamite; textile mills have closed because they cannot get funds to import wool tops and dyes. The sinking state of Turkey's credit has scared off foreign enterprisers who might otherwise have taken advantage of Menderes' generous terms for new oil and other foreign investors.

The cost of living has been rising 30 per cent a year for the last three years. Coffee is almost unobtainable. Hardships are greatest in the cities, where a laborer must work three days to buy a pair of shoes, and a tourist at the bar of the new Istanbul Hilton Hotel pays six liras—almost a workingman's entire one-day pay—for a martini.

Inflation and the lopsided boom have bred many millionaires. But Turkey's trouble has mostly bred deep discontent. It boiled viciously to the surface . . . in the Istanbul and Izmir riots [in September 1955]. They began, ironically, in what was almost certainly a government-inspired plan for demonstrations against Greece's claims to Cyprus. But before the nasty surge was checked, it had swept beyond minorities, to strike at many Turks as well—a raging protest against high prices, low wages, and the sight of luxury in its midst. . . .

Premier Menderes reacted in a manner characteristic of autocrats, but puzzling for one duly elected and reelected by great majorities and seemingly backed by 500 of the 541 delegates in Parliament. He blamed the whole thing on the Communists, summoned the Assembly to approve a state of martial law. It was not, however, the first demonstration of Democrat Menderes' liberties with democratic procedure. Under its repressive, criticism-squelching 1954 press law, the Menderes regime has arrested some 40 journalists. The once independent judiciary has been placed under the public prosecutor's thumb.

Thirty years of Turkish politics have calloused any soft spots in Menderes' disposition. Born to cotton-planting wealth (in a family that took its name from the River Meander of classic fame), he studied at the American College in Izmir, took a law degree but has never practiced. Menderes dislikes criticism—none of his original cabinet has survived in the same office. "Anybody who shows any spirit goes out," says a British observer. . . .

Those concerned with Turkey's sore plight wish that the Premier had shown himself as diligent in dealing with Turkey's deepening economic crisis as in dealing with his critics. They attribute much of this inconsistency to the man whom Menderes has chosen to direct economic affairs, a suave and resourceful protégé named Fatin Rustu Zorlu.

Zorlu is an ambitious, Paris-schooled diplomat who has risen swiftly to the posts of Deputy Premier and Acting Foreign Minister by his talent for improvising debt settlements, spouting statistics, and providing his boss with arguments to show that Turkey's economic situation is basically shipshape. Turkey's foreign-exchange deficits, Zorlu explains, are paltry little imbalances caused by the passing inconvenience of a couple of drought-shriveled harvests in a row. All the country needs is a "fund of maneuver," say $300 million, to see it through till the development program starts paying off around 1958. This, Zorlu insists, is where the United States should step in with its purse. Says Zorlu: "Turkey is confident of itself. We can overcome our difficulties even alone—but we will arive more quickly if we are aided." . . .

The United States has poured more than $1.5 billion in military and economic aid into Turkey since 1948—with no regrets, and, indeed, with results that speak well for Turkey. Stoutly anti-Communist well before the Western countries awoke to the extent of the U.S.S.R. menace, Turkey plunged resolutely into beefing up its army, sent a valiant 4,500-man brigade and replacements to Korea, accepted and promoted John Foster Dulles' concept of the "Northern Tier" alliance.

All this stout performance merely made it harder for United States officials to give their answer when Zorlu arrived in Washington last summer and formally held out his hand. The State Department had come generally to the . . . conclusion . . . that Turkey's present course leads to bankruptcy. Additional United States millions, Zorlu was told, would merely stay the day, and Turkey would be back in a matter of months for more. When United States Treasury Secretary George Humphrey went to Turkey . . . for the World Bank meeting, he put the United States position directly to Menderes himself.

Not even the tough No of tough George Humphrey swayed Adnan Menderes. Having . . . turned down the advice of its ally, the Turkish Government called in yet another adviser to give it the benefit of his advice and his knowledge of the ways of United States Government. As the legal counsel to the Turkish Government in the United States, . . . Manhattan lawyer Thomas E. Dewey has already taken a look at Turkey's economic affairs. . . . Turkey seems to expect that in return for his retainer—$150,000—Tom Dewey will be able to turn a loud No into a multimillion-dollar Yes. But Dewey carefully cleared his plans with the State Department before taking on the assignment, and he was told that the best service he could render his client would be to show them why the United States answer must continue to be No.

Obviously, some very tough people have come to a very tough impasse. The Turks seem confident that they can outstare the United States. The United States is staring back, in the belief that Adnan Menderes will be the first to blink and give ground. [As of September 1956, the loan referred to above had not been granted to Turkey.—Ed.]

CYPRUS: DEFENSE VS. NATIONALISM [7]

Since one of the West's main objectives is to keep the U.S.S.R. out of the Eastern Mediterranean, the issue of the future status of the island of Cyprus, bitterly contested between Britain and Greece, gains in importance as the situation in that area of paramount strategic and political significance deteriorates.

Britain disregards the will of the Greek population of Cyprus who want union with Greece, and holds on forcibly to the island, because various defense systems guarding the Eastern Mediterranean are in the process of collapsing. As the first line of defenses crumbles, or proves ineffectual, from the Suez Canal to Jordan, Britain seeks to protect economic and military interests in the Middle East on which its survival may depend, by taking its stand on Cyprus, its only remaining important base in the Eastern Mediterranean.

The question is whether this policy creates more problems than it solves. The February 19 [1956] elections in Greece were both a reflection of recent events in the area and a reaction against them. . . . The vote has revealed, however, the full measure of Greek sentiment over the Cyprus issue and has shown that nationalism, in Greece as elsewhere, will not bow to strategic considerations.

The apparent cleavage between the military preoccupations of the West and rising nationalism is responsible for a situation which has proved untenable not only in Cyprus but also in other parts of the Eastern Mediterranean and in French North Africa. Efforts to stamp nationalism out as detrimental to military necessity drives the nationalists to consider military necessity the stumbling block to the realization of their plans, and to turn for relief to the U.S.S.R. or, more often, to neutralism. This cleavage creates a vicious circle. When the foundation of defensive alignments is weakened, the West accentuates its intransigence. Intransigence nurtures an increasingly violent, often

[7] From article by Mario Rossi, correspondent on Middle Eastern affairs for the *Christian Science Monitor*. *Foreign Policy Bulletin*. 35:105-6. April 1, 1956. Reprinted by permission.

bloody, form of nationalism. Violence leads to repressions, until one of the two sides is forced to give way but not before the situation has deteriorated dangerously. . . .

Recent events have shown that in a showdown between military considerations and nationalist aspirations, the latter usually prevail. But meanwhile the Cyprus issue has cast a shadow over Greece's attitude to the West, has caused a rift in the Western alliance, has favored Soviet ambitions, and has placed a new "colonial" item on the United Nations agenda.

Divergent political attitudes over the fate of the island have rekindled the traditional hostility between Greece and Turkey, which had subsided after two world wars. Two issues are at stake. First, Ankara claims that since Turkey controlled Cyprus at the time of its cession to Britain in 1878, the island, if relinquished by the British, should revert to Turkey, not to Greece. Second, even if the British stay, Turkey opposes the measure of self-government demanded by the Cypriotes, for fear it might jeopardize the position of the island's 100,000 Turkish minority in a population of 500,000.

As a result of these conflicts the Balkan alliance joining Greece and Turkey with Yugoslavia, which was concluded in August 1954, is deeply split and survives in name only. Turkey, a Middle Eastern country and a member of the Asian-African bloc at the United Nations, has consequently turned more and more decidedly toward the West, while Greece, the cradle of Western civilization, is turning for support to the anticolonial countries of Asia and Africa. Britain was not at first averse to a dispute between Greece and Turkey which would divert the spotlight from its role in Cyprus. The political advantage, however, was transitory because the weakening of the Balkan alliance was followed, further south in the alignment of Eastern Mediterranean defenses, by the inability of the Baghdad Pact to attract Arab League countries and to keep the U.S.S.R. out of the Middle East. King Hussein's dismissal on March 2 [1956] of British Lieutenant General John Bagot Glubb as commander of Jordan's Arab Legion, has dashed hopes that the Baghdad

Pact might become an effective link in the chain of Western defenses, thus forcing Britain to tighten its grip still further over Cyprus.

In the dispute with Britain and Turkey, both members of the Baghdad Pact, Greece has entered Middle Eastern politics by supporting and seeking support from Egypt, a neutralist country with pronounced anti-Western views. Since Yugoslavia, too, has established close links with Egypt and has declared its opposition to the Baghdad Pact, an interaction has developed between events in the Balkans and in the Middle East which was not foreseen when the defense alliances were originally drawn.

The Russians profit by the instability along their southern borders. In both Greece and Cyprus, as in Asia and the Arab world, they apply the tactics of supporting nationalism in its opposition to the strategic considerations of the West. In the UN they also champion the right of peoples to self-determination, while the West, divided against itself, sacrifices principles to expediency. The arrest and deportation on March 9 of Archbishop Makarios, spokesman for Cyprus nationalists, enable Russia, as had often been the case during the last century, to underline its solidarity as an Orthodox country with the aspirations of the Orthodox churches in Cyprus, Greece and the Middle East.

Greece's hostile attitude toward the West is an important factor in the general weakening of Western defenses in the Eastern Mediterranean. Most observers agree that the elections were indicative of popular resentment not only against Britain but also against the United States for its failure to give Greece positive support. The elections were apparently an emotional outburst of popular feelings and should not be interpreted as a swing toward closer ties with the U.S.S.R. Greece could not easily forget the ravages of the civil war with the Communists nor the children the Greek Communists sent to satellite countries during the civil war and who were never returned. But no observer would dare predict what the long-range implications might prove to be should the Greeks become convinced that the accession of Cyprus to their country is to be indefinitely postponed.

THE KEY ISSUE OF OIL [8]

The long-term outlook in the Middle East is dark. Even if an Israel-Arab war is prevented and the truce is enforced, a long struggle for settlement that may last decades is ahead. The Middle East conflict is a part of the Cold War, and no final settlement is possible until real coexistence is reached between the Communist bloc and the West.

This is reflected inside the Arab world, which has divided into two camps. On one side are the Arab leaders who want to cooperate with the West for economic development and defense against Moscow's imperialism. Lined up against them, led by Egypt's Gamal Abdel Nasser, are the Arab leaders who hope to use Soviet power as a lever to eliminate Britain's influence in the Middle East forever.

Western oil companies are caught right in the middle of this rivalry. No matter how they try to avoid it, they are deeply involved. . . .

If you look at the map, you can see what a Middle East war might do to the flow of oil from the Arab countries. More than a quarter of the area's production moves to market through pipelines of the Iraq Petroleum Company and the Arabian American Oil Company (Aramco) to ports in the eastern Mediterranean. If a general war breaks out between the Arabs and the Israelis, these pipelines will be in danger. The IPC lines run through Syria, the area's most unstable country, where the Communists have their best organization in the Middle East. Farther south, Aramco's tapline runs within a few hundred yards of the Israeli-Syrian border.

In the 1948 Arab-Israeli War, IPC's pipeline through Syria— much smaller than the present installation—kept on operating, and there was no interference in the oil fields in Iraq and the Persian Gulf. But most Middle East observers believe that situation would change in a new conflict. Extremist Arab agents are known to be active in various areas—in British-controlled Bahrein, and even in feudal Saudi Arabia. . . .

[8] From "Western Oil Interests Get Caught in the Crossfire." *Business Week.* p 160+. April 21, 1956. Reprinted by permission.

Suez Problem

A still greater problem posed for the oil companies and the West . . . is what happens at the Suez Canal. About one third of Middle East oil moves from the Persian Gulf by tanker around Arabia, through the Red Sea and Suez, and on to Europe and the United States. . . .

If Suez were closed to shipping, oil would have to be carried nearly twice as far, from the Persian Gulf to Western Europe around Africa. There are not enough tankers to do this job. . . .

Europe would have to cut back oil consumption and import oil along a shorter route from the Western Hemisphere. That would mean a heavy drain on United States supplies. Last year the United States imported about 10 per cent of its oil needs from Venezuela. In an emergency the United States would have to give up part of these imports—in addition to the present imports from the Middle East.

What this would do to the United States oil market remains problematical. The experts differ, but the United States petroleum industry is now operating at something between 600,000 and 2 million barrels a day under maximum capacity. Part of this excess production capacity resulted from pressure by the military as a defense measure, and part from the desire of state oil conservation agencies to keep United States wells at their most efficient rate of production.

In an emergency, as during 1951 and early 1952 when 6 per cent of the world's oil supply was cut off by the nationalization of Iranian petroleum, . . . United States producers were able to step in quickly to fill the gap.

Certainly this move would mean a sharp increase in oil prices (United States basic crude prices are about $1 a barrel higher than at the Persian Gulf). Government oil controls like those of World War II could probably not be avoided.

United States exports to Western Europe and diversion of Venezuelan oil to European markets, however, wouldn't solve Britain's problem. Not only would it be difficult for Britain to get the supplies it needs from the Western Hemisphere, but it would also mean dollar expenditures for Britain's largest import now coming from the sterling area. That kind of burden thrown onto the already overtaxed British economy would be catastrophic.

This prospect explains why London has taken the diplomatic offensive in the Middle East against Cairo. Britain sees building a counter-force as its only answer to Nasser's pan-Arabic drive. That's why Britain is building up the Baghdad Pact. This treaty is a defense alliance among Turkey, Iran, Pakistan, Iraq, and Britain. Originally, it was conceived as a "Northern Tier" of Moslem lands acting as a barrier against Soviet imperialism. Now Britain wants to make it a center of cooperation among the Western and the Arab countries, opposed to Nasser's neutralism between the Communists and the West. . . .

Also the British figure Iraq is a good bet because of the tremendous oil resources that last year brought in almost $300 million in royalties from Iraq Petroleum Company. Unlike Saudi Arabia, Iraq is putting 70 per cent of its steadily increasing oil revenues to work for economic development. In direct contrast, the Saudis spend Aramco's payments for royal high living and anti-British intrigues. Since 1950, Baghdad has put more than $430 million into irrigation and reclamation projects. During the next six years that figure should rise to around $850 million. . . .

United States Policy

But Washington does not want to put all its eggs in the one basket of Iraq and the Baghdad Pact. United States policy . . . is to support the pact in its anti-Communist functions. We have even promised to support its economic functions by contributing toward the pact development fund that the British and Moslem members hope to establish. . . . We [have] joined the pact's economic council. But we will not join the pact proper, nor do we want to get mixed up in the Arab family feud.

This attitude is a logical extension of our general policy in the Middle East crisis. Washington refuses to be provoked into any irrevocable action by Arab excesses, by Israeli fears, or by

British tactical maneuvers. Only an outbreak of war or direct Kremlin intervention will basically alter Washington's policy. . . .

Washington's thinking is along these lines:

As long as there is any hope that Nasser's Egyptian revolution will go a constructive, peaceful way, the State Department will not write Cairo off as the British have done.

The long-range settlement of the Israeli-Egyptian problem will take decades. There is no simple or easy solution.

The United States won't permit Middle Eastern oil to be cut off from Britain and Western Europe. On this point, Washington and London have no differences. But the State Department doesn't want to get committed to safeguarding specific British interests—or directly involved in oil company politics, as the Foreign Office already has become.

It's this last point where London and Washington come closest to a parting of the ways.

Britain is, for example, pushing the claim of the Sheikh of Abu Dhabi to the Buraimi Oasis . . . a God-forsaken corner of the Arabian desert where both Aramco and British oil interests think oil could be found. The dispute has already led to fighting by British-officered troops and soldiers of Saudi Arabia. Mediation in the dispute has broken down.

If some solution isn't found, Washington—despite its determination to keep clear of company squabbles—might turn up on the opposite side from London.

IV. THE ARAB-ISRAELI CONFLICT

EDITOR'S INTRODUCTION

Perhaps the most fateful of all Middle Eastern questions are whether a local war will again emerge between Israel and the Arab states and whether such a conflict would give rise to a violent East-West atomic explosion. Phrased thus, however, the continuing Israeli-Arab struggle is set in a perspective which is often lacking in debate about the issues at stake and in the action taken on the frontiers between Israel and its neighbors. The following articles do not raise all of the controversial points usually brought forth when Israeli-Arab affairs are discussed. In the years since World War II some of the earlier disputes about the establishment of Israel have waned.

True, a state of war still exists between the contestants in the technical sense and general hostilities appear to have been narrowly averted only recently. In this situation the Arab states do not recognize Israel's status as a member of the family of nations. Yet, as the debate has turned from violence into something often less than peaceful coexistence, some opinion even within the Arab nations and certainly in the outside world increasingly tends toward acceptance of the *fact* of Israel. This is brought out in later articles in Section V with respect to current American thinking. Within this context the Arab-Israeli conflict has taken a new turn.

Of most dramatic importance, however, and what may well determine whether the conflict remains local or becomes global is the active intervention, by the sale of arms to Egypt, of the Soviet bloc. For it was announced in Egypt on September 27, 1955, that an Egyptian-Czechoslovakian agreement had been signed to exchange surplus Egyptian cotton for an estimated $80 million worth of arms, to include jet fighters, tanks, submarines and artillery. With this announcement an arms race was on which has stirred controversy in many world capitals. The problem of whether the United States should sell arms to Israel, in turn, has necessarily faced Washington ever since—a policy question debated in two articles in Section V.

The articles below restate the positions of the opposing sides and very briefly touch on the situation which arose as a result of the renewed discussion of the problem in the United Nations in the crisis of early 1956. At the outset a chronology covering the period 1947-1956 is given to orient the reader. In the following two interviews the Prime Minister of Egypt and the former Prime Minister and Foreign Minister of Israel center much of their attention on the arms race that has developed in the area. Next are detailed the efforts made by the United Nations Secretary General on his first 1956 mission to the area. In the editorial that follows a very critical stand is taken regarding the Arabs' handling of their case in the latest United Nations discussion. And this is followed in turn by a look at the problems the United Nations Secretary General faces in continuing his attempt to bring about peace. The last selection suggests that, while war has been averted, real peace is still to be achieved.

PALESTINE CHRONOLOGY: 1947-1956 [1]

The state of Israel was established . . . [in 1948 and] is now at the vortex of a struggle involving the Western world and the Communist bloc. What follows is a chronology of events that led up to the present crisis:

1947

September 26—Britain, ruler of Palestine for twenty-five years, announced she would give up her League of Nations mandate.

November 29—With the support of the United States and Russia, the UN voted to partition the Holy Land into separate Jewish and Arab states. The Arab nations threatened war.

[1] From New York *Times.* p E5. July 8, 1956. Reprinted by permission.

1948

May 15—Israel was proclaimed in the area allotted to it by the UN; the United States extended recognition. Arab planes bombed Israel and Arab armies closed in on the new state. Gradually the Israelis pushed the Arabs back.

1949

February 24—Egypt, and later Jordan, Lebanon and Syria, signed UN-sponsored armistices with Israel. But the armistice did not bring real peace. The Arabs set up diplomatic and economic boycotts against Israel.

1950

May 25—The United States, Britain and France issued a declaration that they would keep the military balance by limiting arms shipments to both the Arabs and Israel and would "take action" to prevent frontier violations.

1951

September 11—The UN Security Council called on Egypt to lift its anti-Israel blockade at the Suez Canal. This and subsequent UN efforts to induce the Arabs to make peace with Israel were rejected. Arab circles became increasingly resentful of the Western powers for supporting Israel.

1953

March 2—President Eisenhower expressed his "concern over [the] deterioration in relations between the Arab nations and the United States" and said he intended "to restore the spirit of confidence and trust which had previously characterized these relations."

October 14-15—In retaliation for a series of Jordanian border raids, the Israelis launched an attack in force against Kibya—the beginning of Israel's tough policy of reprisals in force. Washington and the Security Council censured Israel.

1954

January 22—Over Syrian protests, the Security Council voted to permit Israel to build a power project on the Jordan River. Russia vetoed the resolution. This was Moscow's first open bid for Arab friendship and the first of a series of Soviet vetoes on the Arabs' behalf.

February 27—Lieutenant Colonel Gamal Abdel Nasser became Premier of Egypt.

July 27—Britain agreed to quit the Suez Canal Zone. London and Washington believed this concession would induce Egypt to join a Mideast defense system.

1955

January 22—Egypt convened a meeting of the Arab League to block the projected Mideast defense organization. The Nasser regime insisted that all Arab states remain neutral in the cold war. Iraq defied Cairo and announced it would sign up with the West.

September 27—Nasser announced Egypt would obtain heavy arms from the Communist bloc. The Egyptian-Communist alignment shocked the West and alarmed Israel, but among Arab nations Nasser's prestige skyrocketed.

October 23—Israel began a long series of efforts to induce the United States, Britain and France to sell her heavy arms to match Communist shipments to Egypt. The West was cool.

November 22—Britain, Iraq, Iran, Turkey and Pakistan formally organized the Middle East Treaty Organization as a "northern tier" deterrent to Soviet expansion. To counterbalance METO, Premier Nasser organized the neutralist and anti-Israel "southern tier" bloc of Egypt, Syria and Saudi Arabia and set about inducing Jordan to sign up.

December 11—After Syrian attacks on Israeli fishermen on the Sea of Galilee, the Israelis launched a massive raid on Syrian positions. Israel was toughening her policy to show that, as one official put it, she would not sit "like a rabbit waiting for the

[Arab] snake to get big enough to swallow her." The Security Council sharply censured Israel.

December 19—Britain's efforts to induce Jordan to join METO brought bloody anti-Western rioting in Jordan. London charged Saudi Arabia and Egypt with instigating the riots.

1956

March 2—Jordan ousted the British general, John Bagot Glubb, chief of the British-subsidized Arab Legion. London, angered and humiliated, began to reappraise its Arab policy.

March 12—Nasser's "southern tier" announced it had completed plans for resisting Israel and METO.

March 30—London indicated it was seriously considering arms aid for Israel. So did France.

April 2—Secretary Dulles said the United States would not sell Israel arms for the present but would not object if Britain and France did. Israel was deeply disturbed and disappointed.

April 6—UN Secretary General Dag Hammarskjold left on a "peace mission" for the Arab states and Israel to try to induce both sides to comply with the armistice. He warned the world not to expect "dramatic" results.

THE EGYPTIAN CASE [2]

In this interview at Cairo . . . Egypt's Prime Minister Gamal Abdel Nasser tells why he turned to the Soviet bloc for arms.

Q. Mr. Prime Minister, does the arms deal you have made with Communist Czechoslovakia mean that you no longer feel there is any danger of Soviet military aggression against the Middle East?

A. What we must think of is the security of Egypt. We look at things a lot differently from you Americans. We don't spend our time worrying about a world war, or Russian ag-

[2] From "Where War Threatens Now." *U.S. News & World Report.* 39:48-50. November 4, 1955. Reprinted from *U.S. News & World Report,* an independent weekly news magazine published at Washington. Copyright 1955 United States News Publishing Corporation.

gression, or the struggle between East and West. We are interested in Egypt's security, and Egypt's security today means protection against Israel. . . .

Q. But if Russia ever invaded the Middle East and you were equipped with Soviet-made arms, wouldn't all that equipment be useless to you, since, of course, Russians would cut off the supply of your ammunition and spare parts?

A. We are quite aware of that, but we had no choice. We needed arms. The Israelis have said time and again that they want to expand. They talk of having the area from the Euphrates to the Nile. The Herut Party campaigned in the last elections on a line calling for expansion and were returned to Parliament with more representation than they had before. [Herut, with 15 seats, is second to Mapai with 40 in the 120-seat Knesset.] They are constantly making threats.

We could not get arms from the West, so we got them from the East, without conditions. We waited three years to get arms from the West, but they never came, while the West continued to build up Israel. Our revolution here stemmed from the need in Egypt for arms. If there are no arms coming, there will be another revolution here.

I could be patient until Israeli aggression on the Gaza Strip last February 28, but after that I could no longer be so. I am responsible for all of Egypt's interests, which include the defense of its territory as well as all the other things. So I got arms where I could get them, without conditions.

Q. As I understand it, you could have gotten arms from the United States, couldn't you, if you had agreed to accept a small military mission that would supervise the use of the arms?

A. I refused that. We don't like military missions here. An American mission means American influence. I realize that Tito [President of Yugoslavia] has accepted a mission, so had Iraq and so have other countries. But we can't do it here. We had British missions here for seventy-five years, and now we cannot just substitute an American mission for the British one.

Q. But wasn't that somewhat different? You actually had thousands of British troops on your soil, which is different from having a small military mission—

A. We just don't like missions here—any kind of missions. We had German military missions here and don't like those either.

Q. But do you really believe, Mr. Prime Minister, that if an American military mission is here they will say to you: "Mr. Prime Minister, you must do this, you must do that, you must vote this way in the United Nations, and so on?"

A. Our people would think that having an American mission here would be foreign domination. We didn't throw out a British mission in order to get an American one in its place.

Q. Do you think that Egypt would be running less risk in taking arms from the Soviet bloc and thereby leaving itself defenseless against potential Russian aggression than in accepting a small military mission from a country—the United States— which has no aggressive designs on Egypt?

A. You just don't understand Egypt. For us the danger and the thing to worry about now is Israel, not Russia. We must protect ourselves from Israel first.

It's like going down a road and meeting a man with a pistol, and a little farther on there stands a man with a machine gun. You defend yourself against the man with the pistol. It's not going to do you any good to worry about the man with the machine gun, just because it's a bigger weapon, if the man with the pistol shoots you dead.

Q. But wouldn't it be best to figure out a way of taking care of both dangers?

A. For the past three years, the United States has had a chance to arm Egypt, but it hasn't wanted to do so. Shortly— about three months—after our revolution, I had a talk with your Under Secretary of Defense, who told me the United States would be happy to arm Egypt.

Shortly afterward we sent a military mission to Washington, which sat down and discussed with your military men the things we would need, and we were told that we could get the tanks, artillery and other heavy equipment we asked for. We signed a document—the "short form," I believe you call it—for arms purchases, in which we stated that we would use the arms received for purposes of defense only. We agreed to that.

But, then, despite the promises, nothing happened. We didn't get any of those arms. We received a little small stuff—trucks, ambulances and so on. The Americans told us that we must settle the Suez issue with the British first. Well, after we got that settled, we still didn't get any arms.

After the February Gaza Strip incident there was terrific pressure in the country for arms. So I started negotiating with the Russians, and I called in the American Ambassador and told him so. The British Ambassador also came in, and said that if we went ahead and did such a thing the British wouldn't be able to give us anything—anything at all. Those were threats, which we don't like.

Q. Recently, though, didn't the Americans offer you quite a bit of arms on a cash basis?

A. That was after we told them we were negotiating with the Russians—last June. Then they offered us arms. They offered us $27 million worth, but said that to get them we must pay up right away. Well, I told them that $27 million was exactly the total amount of dollars that we had in the Egyptian treasury. We just couldn't do it.

Q. Wasn't there any possibility of getting it on a credit basis—paying in installments, or something of that sort, or paying in local currency?

A. We asked if it would be possible to pay for it in one of these ways, but we never got an answer.

Q. You were never told "No"?

A. No, we just never got an answer. So we went ahead and signed this agreement with the Russians. I think the United States thought that all the time we were bluffing, but, you see, we weren't bluffing at all.

Q. I note, Colonel Nasser, that you keep referring to your arms agreement with the Russians. I assume that by that you are referring to the agreement to buy arms in Czechoslovakia. Or has there been another agreement on arms with Russia as well?

A. No, no other agreement. I should have been saying "the Soviet bloc."

Q. Do you expect that there will be a need for a further agreement, or will this agreement with Czechoslovakia be enough? To put it another way, with the arms you expect to receive under this one agreement with Czechoslovakia, do you believe that the Egyptian army will have at least caught up to Israel—making up for that difference in armed strength that you say has been existing between Egypt and Israel?

A. Oh, yes, certainly. With these arms, we will be all right.

Q. You'll have enough?

A. Yes, we'll have enough.

Q. Mr. Prime Minister, you have often complained about what you call the West's failure to adhere to the balance-of-power principle in its dispatch of arms to Israel and the world. Do you agree, though, that the principle is a good one—that Israel and the Arab countries should be given equal amounts of equipment?

A. No, I cannot see the justice in equating Israel with the entire Arab world. Israel has only about 1.7 million people, and Egypt alone has more than 20 million.

Q. You think, then, Egypt alone should have at least as much in the way of arms as Israel?

A. Yes. We have to be in a position to defend our territory alone. We cannot count on the support of the other Arab countries. There is no joint Arab command, no joint military planning among the Arab states. If Israel should attack us in force, we cannot necessarily count on Syria, for example, entering into the war against Israel. We Egyptians must be able to beat back Israel on our own.

Q. Do you mean, then, that you think each country of the Arab area should have forces strong enough so that it could fight the Israelis on an equal basis just on its own, without help from the other Arab countries?

A. Well, of course, for some of the Arab countries that would be economically impossible. Neither Syria nor Lebanon, for example, could possibly become that strong. Their economies could not stand up to it. There is a limit.

You Americans know well yourselves that a strong military potential needs a strong economic base. At the beginning of the last war, for example, it was not the American army that was the strongest but the German. But America, with its great natural resources, its productive capacities, its industrial base and so on, could build up an unbeatable military force within six months or so.

Q. How about Jordan as a military force? We always hear about the famous Arab Legion there—

A. Not at all. Jordan is small and could not put forward the strength to handle Israel on its own. Egypt is a different proposition, however. Egypt has to be in a position to go along alone against Israel. If Egypt falls, the rest of the Arab world is finished, too.

Q. You mentioned a moment ago that there is no joint military planning or military cooperation of any kind in the Arab area. Why is that?

A. Well, the countries of the Arab world have their local differences among themselves.

Q. Do you think your arms agreement with Czechoslovakia is likely to result in more cordial relations between Egypt and Iraq on the issue of arms supply? That is, hasn't Iraq's arms agreement with the United States and its tie-in with Turkey been the cause of some dissension between your two countries?

A. Iraq always used to tell us that to get arms you have to sign a pact. They meant that we have to tie ourselves in with the West on some Middle Eastern defense arrangement against Communist aggression. Well, we didn't. The Iraqis may have different ideas about that now, after we got arms from Czechoslovakia without signing any pact at all or receiving a military mission.

And, as I understand it, Iraq hardly got any of the arms it was supposed to get from the United States. Apparently the item they have received most of is ambulances. I'm sure Ben-Gurion would be delighted to see a long line of ambulances lined up near his frontier. It wouldn't indicate to him that we were very optimistic about our chances. You can't defend a frontier with ambulances. Neither can you with schools and hospitals. I wish we could. But we need arms. We have had to divert much of our effort and money away from things like schools and hospitals so that we can get arms. When this problem has been resolved, we can go back to doing more for Egypt's social progress and the building of the country.

Q. Can you tell me something about the state of Egypt's Army?

A. We have a Regular Army, Reserve and National Guard. The National Guard is composed of volunteers who get trained for a month and then return to their homes. They take periodical training after that. In the event of an emergency, we could mobilize 300,000 National Guardsmen within forty-eight hours.

I want to say that in Egypt we like America and Americans. It was the British who occupied us for so many years, not the Americans. But the United States in recent years has not seemed able to understand our problems and our needs.

THE ISRAELI SIDE [3]

This interview [is] with Israel's [former] Prime Minister Moshe Sharett . . . in Jerusalem. . . .

Q. Mr. Prime Minister, has the Czech arms deal with Egypt increased the danger of war in the Middle East?

A. Very much. Large quantities of arms are usually meant for war and not for peace. We consider Egypt fundamentally bent upon aggression.

We cannot conceive of any other object or purpose for which Egypt would embark upon an expenditure of such magnitude for the acquisition of arms unless it be for launching—at a time

[3] From "Where War Threatens Now." *U.S. News & World Report.* 39:50-4. November 4, 1955. Reprinted from *U.S. News & World Report,* an independent weekly news magazine published at Washington. Copyright 1955 United States News Publishing Corporation.

which Egypt would probably find appropriate—an offensive against Israel in order to wipe it out.

Q. Wasn't Prime Minister Nasser of Egypt taking a calculated risk, when he concluded the Czech arms deal, that Israel might take preventive action to avert an unfavorable shift in the balance of military strength?

A. I don't know how farsighted Colonel Nasser is. It seems that he is extremely shortsighted and living from hand to mouth. To him it was a major piece of self-aggrandizement—for himself and for his clique and for Egypt. And also, because he is violently hostile, he must have thought that one day this will certainly give him a chance of settling old scores with Israel. He is pledged to destroy us—if he can.

Q. If arms aid from the West does not materialize, and you are confronted with a shift in the balance of military power in favor of Egypt, wouldn't Israel feel obligated to take preventive action before Egypt was too strong—that is, force a military showdown with Egypt?

A. I would not attempt to cross that bridge before I got to it. I saw this idea expressed in the foreign press. Apparently, newspapers think it is inherent in the logic of the situation. I would very ardently wish that we should not be driven to resort to that kind of a short cut to our security.

Q. Colonel Nasser claims he was obliged to get arms from the Soviet bloc because he couldn't get them from the West, and he claims further that the French were diverting to Israel arms ordered by Egypt—

A. But, as things stood before he concluded that deal with Czechoslovakia, he had a definite superiority over us in all heavy armament—on land, at sea and in the air. The Czech deal has increased that superiority—I don't know how many times.

Q. In terms of total military capability, doesn't Israel still have an advantage?

A. Israel has a definite advantage in quality—in the quality of its manpower and in its technical and organizational ability to put to better use such weapons as are in its hands. But Israel is always at a disadvantage in numbers of men and in the quantity of its equipment.

There has always been a gap in favor of Egypt, and that gap is about to be increased enormously and very menacingly. Moreover, Egypt has only Israel to settle accounts with, whereas Israel is surrounded by several enemies and has to keep account of them all.

Q. In your opinion, will the Czech arms deal result in a decisive shift in the balance of military power, to the disadvantage of Israel?

A. That is what I have been trying to convey—a decisive shift in the balance of military strength. You may be aware that Egypt's military budget is almost equal to the total budget of Israel—regular and development and security all put together.

Q. Do you feel that the arms Egypt is receiving from Czechoslovakia eventually will overcome Israel's qualitative superiority?

A. Definitely. I feel very much that will be the case, unless Israel succeeds in increasing very considerably its own armaments. But Israel will find itself terribly handicapped by lack of financial resources in trying to achieve that.

Q. Is this the beginning of a continuing arms race?

A. This is an enormous step forward in the arms race. It gives it a tremendous impetus. It has started a new cycle—a new and much broader cycle—in the arms race.

I have already taken exception to the United States military-aid agreement with Iraq, but after that treaty was concluded there was no further progress in supplying arms to the Arab states. That is to say, that process was partially arrested when the Soviet Union suddenly injected itself into the picture and completely revolutionized the situation.

Q. You have pointed out that Israel at present has a qualitative superiority over Egypt, but that Czech arms might cause a decisive shift in the military balance. Isn't Israel obliged to act to prevent that from happening, in view of your belief that Colonel Nasser is out to destroy this country?

A. This decisive shift is a calamity for Israel, and anyone tries to prevent a calamity.

Q. Do you see any possibility of getting arms for Israel from the Soviet bloc, as Nasser is doing for Egypt?

A. We shall in the first instance turn West and see what we can get there, because the Western powers are under an obligation which they voluntarily assumed through the so-called tripartite declaration of 1950 (by United States, Britain, France) to see to it that the balance of military strength in the Middle East is not upset.

It is, therefore, we believe, up to them to bring us up to some point where the gap will at least be appreciably reduced, if not altogether eliminated.

Q. Has Israel made any approach whatever to Russia or any of the satellites for arms?

A. No. I would like to point out that, according to our information, it was the Soviet Union which in the first instance made overtures to Egypt and to some other Arab countries.

Q. Has Russia or any of the satellites approached Israel, formally or informally, with an offer of arms or a hint that arms might be available if Israel asked?

A. The answer is in the negative. There has been no approach whatsoever from government to government—none at all.

Q. You said that Israel would turn to the West for arms, initially—

A. If the situation goes from bad to worse, and we are desperately in need of further arms to save our state and our lives, we shall naturally look for arms wherever we can find them.

Q. If ultimately you felt compelled to seek arms from the Russians, do you see any possibility that they would supply them?

A. I don't know. The contingency has not arisen, and they haven't been put to the test.

Q. In your opinion, what is Russia's purpose in offering arms to Egypt?

A. At least, to establish a foothold in the Middle East.

Q. Do you think that the Russians might agree to curb the flow of arms to Egypt if the Western powers included them in the tripartite agreement you mentioned earlier—in other words, if they were given a voice in Middle East affairs?

A. It is not for me to forecast.

Q. But do you think that a four-power agreement on the Middle East, including Russia, would give Israel greater security than the present tripartite agreement which excluded Russia?

A. Not if there is no unity of purpose among the four. For the time being I don't see evidence of it. I see evidence to the contrary. There is no use combining powers in a joint guarantee if they are going to be at loggerheads with one another.

The question is: What is Russia interested in? Is she interested in stability or is she interested in a state of precarious unbalance? I don't know.

Q. What significance do you see in the fact it was the Russians who made the original overture in negotiations for delivery of Czech arms to Egypt?

A. The Soviet Union was probably aiming at establishing a position for itself in the Middle East to counteract the effort of the United States and other Western democracies to build up the sector in this area of their world defenses. However, the Soviet Union could not be unaware of the fact that Egypt could not possibly be described as a peace-loving nation in view of its obstinate and vehement refusal to make peace with Israel, which refusal is constantly accentuated by acts of war on her part.

I could say that this whole move, to my mind, stands in flagrant contradiction to the "Geneva spirit." Russia has embarked upon a policy of striving to reduce and eliminate international tension, pave the way for permanent stability and peace throughout the world. Here it has acted as a factor upsetting the existing stability and exposing peace within the Middle East to a very serious threat.

Q. What can the United States do to counter this Russian attempt to penetrate the Middle East?

A. It is really for them to say. What we, Israel, are primarily concerned about is our security.

Q. Do you favor an effort by the United States to persuade Russia to call off the arms deal with Egypt?

A. Definitely. Speaking the other night, I said that one still hopes against hope that the Soviet Union, on realizing the enormity of the step that they have taken, will desist from this disastrous course.   Nevertheless, we must be prepared for the worst, and very quickly.

Q. Do you think it is possible for the United States to persuade Colonel Nasser to cancel the Czech arms deal in exchange for arms from the West?

A. I am not a prophet.   For the time being, I see that the United States is not showing an inclination to engage in that form of action of competing with Russia in offering arms to Egypt.   For the time being, they are not showing this tendency. What they will do I don't know.

Q. But do you think an offer of that sort by the United States would be effective?

A. Again I can't say.   Nasser may get the best of both worlds, and his superiority to us may become cumulative.

Q. If neither Russia nor Egypt can be persuaded to call off this arms deal, then you feel that the Western powers should supply arms to Israel?

A. Arms and a security pact both.   The two must go together.   The security pact is very important, but it is not in itself a complete and absolute guarantee.

Q. And these arms from the West would be required on a large scale?

A. Fairly large, yes.   I think these recent developments have revolutionized our conception as to the quantity and the kind of arms that we need.

Q. How can Israel finance an arms program of that magnitude?

A. It is really a tragic prospect to be faced with this compulsion of diverting very limited resources from most urgent tasks of economic development to the acquisition of arms.   But one has to worry first and foremost about one's safety—that is to say, about one's survival—before one can think of progress and development.   Therefore it will have to be done.   It is a terrible pity.   That is why we have been all the time most emphatic in opposing any arms race in the Middle East.

We said to the Western powers: "Don't give arms either
to the Arabs or to ourselves, but naturally if you give arms to
the Arabs you must give to us—though we would prefer your
not giving to either, in order to prevent an arms race."

Q. Do you think the American attempt to form the "northern tier" defense alignment in the Middle East is a sensible
approach to the problem of resisting Russian encroachment in
the area?

A. On the face of it, from America's point of view, yes.
But we would have wished that it did not include Iraq, because
Iraq again is a state hostile to us and therefore an enemy.

Iraq is an enemy of internal peace in the Middle East. They
show implacable hostility to Israel and fanatical determination
to maintain a state of war between the countries of the Arab
League and ourselves. Therefore we did not consider Iraq a
suitable partner for joining any scheme of over-all Middle Eastern defense, and we regarded the military-aid agreement concluded between the United States and Iraq as very reprehensible,
inimical to our safety and to the internal stability of the Middle
East.

Q. But would it be possible to build an effective defense
grouping in the Middle East without Iraq?

A. I see that Turkey is in, Iran is in and Pakistan is in—
and they are countries further north than Iraq.

Q. Did the arms Iraq received from the United States under
this aid agreement upset the arms balance between Israel and
the Arab states?

A. Inasmuch as Iraq is an enemy of Israel and joins in the
cause of promising a second round—yes.

Q. But the upset in the military balance was not serious
enough for you to regard it as a real threat?

A. Anyhow, the new imbalance is much more serious than
that former imbalance. First, because it concerns a country
adjoining Israel and in an active state of war with Israel. Iraq
is not "on the borders of Israel." It is a little further away.

But Egypt is on our border and has been engaged in active
war against us. They have been sending terrorist bands deep
into our territory, violating the armistice agreement in many

other respects and now blockading the approach to our southern port of Eilat [Elath]—preventing all Israeli ships from entering the Gulf [of Aqaba] there. They have put an embargo on Israeli shipping through the Suez Canal.

Q. How do you explain the fact that Colonel Nasser in recent months has adopted this much tougher line toward Israel?

A. He has suffered a number of setbacks. I think the starting point was the conclusion of the pact between Turkey and Iraq which has wrested the balance of leadership very emphatically to the side of Iraq.

He then tried to form, as a counterpart to that pact—to offset it—a tripartite military alliance between Egypt, Syria and Saudi Arabia, to offset the Turko-Iraqi pact. He failed in that enterprise. Syria wouldn't join him. Didn't, anyhow, at the time. That was his second failure.

Then a third setback which he experienced and which was very wounding to his *amour-propre* [self-esteem] was on the Sudan issue. In the Sudan, tendencies have asserted themselves of not merging with Egypt, of maintaining and developing Sudan's separate independence—political and economic.

You must always remember that Nasser's position within Egypt is not a very firmly entrenched one. There is no popular basis whatsoever for his government. It is a military junta which apparently believes that it can only maintain its position by military extravagance—by making a show of force. That is my attempt to rationalize Nasser's behavior. The very fact of defying the Western powers is enhancing his prestige in Egypt, and throughout the Arab world in which neutralist tendencies are so prevalent.

Q. Why did he use the Israel issue—what he called "the threat from Israel"—to justify the Czech arms deal?

A. He has used the Israel issue as a cover, as a convenient excuse in order to impart to this move the semblance of defense and not aggression.

Q. In your opinion, will Colonel Nasser's bid for leadership of the Arab world lead him to consider war with Israel?

A. I think that is the inevitable course of logic. His ambition is to annihilate Israel.

THE UNITED NATIONS CEASE-FIRE [4]

The cease-fire agreement between Egypt and Israel, announced on April 19 [1956] by UN Secretary General Hammarskjold, constituted a first step toward enforcing compliance with the four general armistice agreements of 1949 between Israel and the bordering Arab states: Egypt, Jordan, Lebanon, and Syria. Hammarskjold had been sent to the Middle East, under a resolution unanimously adopted by the Security Council on April 4 [1956], on an urgent mission to reduce tensions threatening international peace. He was directed to conduct a survey of various aspects of enforcement and compliance with the 1949 armistice terms, and to "arrange with the parties for the adoption of any measures which . . . he considers would reduce existing tensions along the armistice demarcation lines."

In effect, the cease-fire between Egypt and Israel represented little more than a new truce on the truce line—a promise by the two countries to honor the armistice they had solemnly pledged to observe seven years before. Nevertheless, it was hoped that if the agreement, and those later reached with Syria, Jordan, and Lebanon, were faithfully carried out, it would be possible to proceed with wider negotiations looking toward general stabilization.

The armistice which Israel and the neighboring Arab states undertook to respect in 1949 specifically prohibited any "warlike or hostile acts" along the 600 miles of demarcation lines established by the agreements. . . .

The 1949 armistice terms were not imposed by the United Nations, but were the product of direct negotiations conducted under the auspices of Ralph J. Bunche, then serving as mediator for the Security Council. The provisions were framed by the countries themselves. It was declared in the preamble of each agreement that the purpose was "to facilitate the transition from the present truce to permanent peace in Palestine." To supervise the agreements, mixed armistice commissions were established on

[4] From "Middle East Commitments," by William T. Stone, editor, *Editorial Research Reports*. *Editorial Research Reports*. no 18:349-52. May 9, 1956. Reprints by permission.

each frontier, composed of representatives of the two governments concerned, with a neutral chairman appointed by the Chief of Staff of the UN Truce Supervision Organization.

The area to be occupied by Israel under the armistice agreements was almost one third larger than that allocated to the Jewish state in the 1947 plan for partition of Palestine. (The partition plan, adopted by the General Assembly November 29, 1947, had called for a Jewish state, an Arab state, and an international regime for the city of Jerusalem, all within an economic union.) The partition plan, objectionable to the Jews, was totally unacceptable to the Arab states and could not be carried into effect by the United Nations. Consequently, the demarcation lines assigned to each country in the main the territories controlled by its armies when the fighting ceased. The lines were not regarded as permanent boundaries; the task of reaching a final territorial settlement was left for future negotiation.

UN Efforts to Enforce Truce Provisions

The United Nations has been dealing with problems growing out of the Arab-Israeli conflict almost continuously since the armistice agreements were signed. The Security Council has met on the Palestine question more than ninety times since 1949 in efforts to obtain observance of the truce provisions. The General Assembly and other UN agencies have attempted to cope with basic political and economic problems left unresolved at the end of the Arab-Israeli war. Numerous proposals have been advanced in the UN and elsewhere for settlement of specific issues.

Despite recurring border incidents, resumption of open warfare was avoided during the first six years of the truce, and some progress was made in the field of economic cooperation. Yet at the beginning of 1956 the prospect of a general settlement of Arab differences with Israel seemed more remote than at any time since 1949.

No Arab nation had recognized the Jewish state, and the Arab boycott of Israel had been intensified. Egypt had denied passage of Israeli ships through the Suez Canal on the ground that "a state of war" existed between the two countries. The problem of repatriation or relocation of 900,000 Arab refugees from Palestine had grown more acute from year to year. Frontier violence had increased and the task of enforcing compliance with the armistice agreements had become more difficult.

In dealing with frontier violence, the UN mixed armistice commissions had little independent authority to police the demarcation lines and were dependent on local agreements which were broken repeatedly by both sides. Numerous incidents were taken to the Security Council, and both sides were repeatedly censured for violations of the truce. The Council censured Israel last year for a particularly flagrant violation of the armistice with Egypt, and recommended urgent measures to strengthen the UN Truce Organization.

General E. L. M. Burns, Canadian Chief of Staff of the UN Truce Organization, attempted to work out agreements between Israel and Egypt for maintenance of joint patrols along sensitive sections of the demarcation lines, for manning of outposts by regular troops, and for local commanders' policing arrangements. Some of those measures were put into effect for a time, but the agreements failed to hold against mounting tension this spring.

Secretary General's Mission and Chances for Peace

In an interim report to the UN Security Council on May 3 [1956] Secretary General Hammarskjold observed that the new cease-fire agreements between Israel and the surrounding Arab states represented an important advance over earlier local agreements and constituted "recognition . . . of the obligation to observe a fundamental principle of the Charter." Hammarskjold said:

I wish to draw attention to the difference in character between previous cease-fires, which have been established locally or between military commanders, and a cease-fire of the character envisaged in my negotiations. The cease-fire I have aimed at under my mandate from the Security Council is one governed by a reaffirmation by the governments, given to the United Nations, to comply unconditionally with the fundamental clause of the various armistice agreements, and establishes anew the legal situation on which the armistice regime was to be founded. It furthermore expresses a recognition in this particular situation of the obligation to observe a fundamental principle of the Charter.

Each of the new cease-fire agreements, Hammarskjold conceded, included "a reservation as to self-defense"; however, he added that his negotiations with all of the governments concerned had been "concluded with positive results."

AN EDITORIAL VIEW [5]

The United Nations Security Council has . . . [spent tedious hours] wrestling with the wording of a British resolution that expressed hope for a lasting peace in Palestine. The delay that kept the Council working overtime was due mainly to the reluctance of the Arab states—Lebanon, Syria, Jordan and Egypt —to admit that the State of Israel legally exists and to give up, for good and all, their ambition to drive the Israelis into the Mediterranean. . . .

Not one Arab speaker said one word to indicate that he felt the awful responsibility of restoring or maintaining peace in the Near East; not one showed the slightest understanding, or desire to understand, the urge that drove so many abused and harassed individuals into the ancient land of Palestine, to set up a new commonwealth and labor for a new hope; not one welcomed the kind of peace that might result from accepting Israel as a neighbor; each, without exception, seemed to be waiting for the ultimate catastrophe that by wrecking the Mediterranean world, and perhaps all the Western world, might destroy the tiny State of Israel.

These assertions are not rhetorical. The fault the Arabs found with the original British resolution was that it used words suggesting, however vaguely, that a peaceful and permanent settlement of the trouble between Israel and her Arab neighbors might be reached. The Arab spokesmen wouldn't have this. They regarded it as an offense for the United Nations to endorse, or the

[5] From "The Truth about Palestine," editorial. New York *Times.* p 18. June 2, 1956. Reprinted by permission.

Secretary General to attempt, any solution that might put an end to the suffering and suspense in the Near East and open the way to peace and prosperity for all. They stuck to medieval notions that are now as out of date as chain armor, spears and battle-axes.

Listen to the Syrian spokesman, Ambassador Ahmad el-Shukairy, speaking. . . . He referred to Palestine—that is, the State of Israel, recognized by our own and most other governments, received in 1949 as a member of the United Nations—as "part and parcel of the Arab homeland." He went on to say:

> To advocate the idea of a mutually acceptable solution must inevitably lead to a reversal of all the resolutions of the United Nations. . . . We must begin from the beginning. We must start *de novo* on a clean sheet. Everything written by the United Nations should be written off, ever since the 29th November 1947. [This was the date of the UN partition resolution.] The establishment of Israel, its membership in the United Nations and all other resolutions will have to be revoked. Then, and then only, the United Nations can look forward to a solution "on a mutually acceptable basis."

We have to put this remarkable utterance into the context of a debate over Mr. Hammarskjold's patient and impartial efforts to stop the killing in the Near East. Mr. Hammarskjold reported, as in duty bound. He had kept—so it seemed to most observers—within the limits of the April 4 resolution, under which he had gone to Palestine. He had received assurances from all the parties, the four Arab states necessarily included, that they would try to reduce border squabbles and accept an increased and improved measure of UN supervision. There is every indication that the Arab states and Israel gave the assurances in good faith. But if we judge by the Arab arguments in the Security Council this week this good faith was in the Arab case of a temporary nature. Given an opportunity, one had to conclude, the Arabs would pounce on Israel.

Neither side in the Near Eastern troubles has been without blame. Each side has unnecessarily taken innocent lives. But the Israelis are now willing to settle and end the bloodshed. The Arabs, if their spokesmen truly represented them this week, are not ready to do this finally and for all time.

PROBLEMS FOR THE UN SECRETARY GENERAL [6]

Despite Dag Hammarskjold's continued optimism, the net effect of the recent Security Council debate was to strengthen misgivings about the ultimate outcome of the Palestine situation.

The Security Council cannot compel any nation to accept any kind of settlement. Even in theory, the most it can do is to intervene to prevent or stop hostilities.

Since the Security Council's powers are thus limited, it consistently has endorsed peaceful settlements, on a mutually acceptable basis, that is. How else, short of war, can there be a settlement?

Yet the Security Council, out of deference to the Arab states and the Soviet Union, has eliminated its standard endorsement of a "mutually acceptable" settlement from its latest Palestine resolution. In fairness to the other members of the Council, it has to be emphasized that the British delegation, which introduced the resolution, was primarily responsible. The United States and France both opposed the deletion.

It can only be assumed that Sir Anthony Eden, British Prime Minister, and Selwyn Lloyd, British Foreign Secretary, wanted to make one more attempt to conciliate the Arabs. In recent months the British had advocated a tougher line to the Arabs.

The British have returned to their earlier position. It may be surmised that the British included the phrase originally because the Soviet delegate, to the annoyance of the Arabs, recently had endorsed a "mutually acceptable" settlement. Perhaps the British hoped their action might help drive a wedge between the Arabs and their friends in Moscow.

Whatever the motive, the aftermath was unfortunate. It did two things.

First, it drew attention to the increased demands of the Arabs, whose minimum price for a settlement now includes full compliance by Israel with the partition resolution, and thereby gave

[6] From "UN Secretary Renews Mideast Peace Moves," by Thomas J. Hamilton, chief UN correspondent of the New York *Times*. New York *Times*. p E3. June 10, 1956. Reprinted by permission.

the Soviet Union a chance to reconfirm its solidarity with them at negligible cost.

Second, it once more brought into the open the disputes among the Western powers, which are responsible for the continued absence of a policy.

The only recourse for the Security Council, therefore, was to do what it did: to compliment the Secretary General of the United Nations on his mission to the Middle East and ask him to continue his good offices. Certainly the situation is calmer now than it was three months ago, when the Council asked him to go to the Middle East to improve armistice conditions.

Under the renewed Security Council mandate Mr. Hammarskjold will not return to the Middle East. Moreover, he still is limited to an attempt to improve the local situation by reaching agreements for the prevention or detection of frontier incidents. In response to protests from the Arab nations and the Soviet Union, the United States dropped the attempt to obtain wider powers for Mr. Hammarskjold's original assignment, and Britain did the same when the identical problem came up this time.

Under his over-all powers, however, the Secretary General considers that he has a right to try to negotiate a peace settlement, or at least part of one. He gave a clue to the way he was thinking at a news conference two days ago, when he discussed two—and only two—of the issues that certainly would have to be settled before peace could be reached.

These are the refusal of Egypt to permit Israeli ships to pass through the Suez Canal and the plight of the 900,000 Palestine Arab refugees, most of whom are being kept alive on a United Nations dole.

Mr. Hammarskjold is understood to be hopeful that he can help to bring about action not only to alleviate these two problems but also to pave the way for a lasting improvement and an ultimate Arab-Israel peace settlement.

The Suez Canal issue, together with Egypt's interference with access to Elath, Israel's isolated port on the Gulf of Aqaba, is itself a reminder that there is still no peace treaty between the two sides in the Palestine war.

Egypt bases its Suez Canal policy on the fact that Egypt and Israel still are technically at war. The Security Council rejected this contention in 1951, and vainly called on Egypt to remove the restrictions. For the last two years, however, goods consigned to and from Israel have been allowed to pass through the canal provided they were carried on vessels not owned by Israelis.

Israel has complained to the Security Council that Egypt has used indirect means to prevent a Greek freighter, carrying cement from Haifa to Elath from going through the canal. If the Egyptian Government is reverting to the old practice Mr. Hammarskjold's chances of persuading it to remove the restrictions would appear to be slim.

Before the Soviet Union intervened in the Middle East the refugee problem was the fundamental issue, and even now it is the most important local problem. The return of all the refugees was only one of the demands made by Ahmad el-Shukairy, Syrian delegate to the United Nations. Shukairy is a Palestine Arab who had to give up his law practice in Jerusalem because of the Palestine war.

In the present circumstances the Arab states will demand that Israel permit the return of most of the refugees, at least, and compensate those not allowed to return for their property. Since Israel objects that their return would mean the entrance of a powerful fifth column, and that it does not have the money to pay compensation, the difficulty of finding a solution is obvious.

Until now, efforts to solve the refugee problem have been linked with plans for the development of the Jordan River . . . and with a compromise territorial settlement.

In the past the United States has made repeated offers to help finance such a settlement. Mr. Hammarskjold, however, is understood to believe that the refugee problem can be reduced to manageable proportions if, after he has time to prepare a plan, the United States would agree to contribute $100 million.

Other United Nations members would be expected to make comparable contributions. If, despite the lowering clouds, the Secretary General should succeed in these two efforts it would be relatively easy to solve the other problems. But nobody can be sure that he will succeed.

"NO DRIFT TO PEACE" [7]

The Middle East crisis seems to be assuming a new aspect. There appears to be less chance of imminent outbreak of full-scale fighting in Palestine but possibly more chance of ultimate war. Britain, France and the United States have tacitly reneged on their 1950 peace pledge by handing prior responsibility back to UN. And—again tacitly—Soviet Russia has been recognized as having both interest and influence in a region from which the West had sought to exclude it. . . .

Soviet intentions must be considered in a new light. There is no longer so clear-cut an alternative of Anglo-French-American military action to forestall or reply to an aggression. M. Pineau, . . . exploring the matter in Moscow, considers the 1950 declaration nullified by new Allied political strategy. While Secretary Dulles claims the French Foreign Minister never said anything so strong to him, he argues the tripartite pledge was always subject to our prior UN obligations.

All three Western powers are clearly relieved to return direct accountability to the Security Council. The United States is unwilling to risk building up Israeli defense forces for fear of offending the Arab bloc and losing oil and base rights. The French are fully occupied militarily with the Algerian revolt. They have little to spare for other emergency commitments. The British might have wished to take a tougher line. But their hands are tied in Cyprus, their nearest offshore base. They hope to induce Moscow to help calm the uneasy situation.

There are no signs yet that Russia is doing more than talk softly about Palestine. Czechoslovak aircraft are still being flown to Egypt. Now, thanks to Greek anger over Cyprus, Athens has granted them permission to refuel en route. There are unconfirmed rumors that the U.S.S.R. is for the first time selling military equipment directly to the Arabs. Twenty Russian transport planes are reportedly on the way to Cairo.

When Bulganin and Khrushchev were in London they admitted the validity of Britain's interest in Middle East petroleum.

[7] From "There is No Drift to Peace in Palestine," by C. L. Sulzberger, columnist. New York *Times*. p 18. May 19, 1956. Reprinted by permission.

They offered to reduce war fever by preventing their orbit from sending more material to Egypt. But the price was that the West must also cease shipping arms. Moscow meant the Baghdad Pact should be abandoned. Britain is not prepared to pay this price. But it is possible the military aspects of that alliance will be increasingly played down.

The atmosphere remains mistrustful. Nobody particularly welcomes our decision not to sell weapons to Israel but to encourage other allies to do so—and to relinquish earmarked equipment for this purpose. Soviet behavior seems to belie harmonious intentions. And the Egyptians appear angry with both Washington and Moscow.

There has been delay in launching Colonel Nasser's grandiose scheme for a high dam at Aswan on the Nile. We have told him help will be forthcoming when he gets agreement on power and water-sharing with the Sudan. But there is no accord as yet between the two Nilotic countries. Nasser feels he is no longer receiving "preferential treatment." Both Cairo and Jerusalem suspect we are thinking of writing off the leader of Egypt's revolution.

The temporarily calming results of the Hammarskjold mission to the Middle East are wearing thin. Israel still desperately seeks striking-force weapons to build up retaliatory power in case of an Arab attack. Jerusalem would like to be able to hit back far behind enemy lines and advertise this as a deterrent against aggression. But, although Foreign Minister Sharett eloquently quoted Dulles' own speeches on such strategy while pleading for arms in Washington, he got nowhere.

The Arab states are worried lest a deal is shaping up between Moscow and the West which would cut off future supplies of Soviet-bloc arms and allow Israel to aright the military balance. This thought stimulates the jingoes. Israel fears that, after the recent allotment of twenty-four French Mystère fighters, its modern defensive power will be frozen; that the Arabs will gain more Communist weapons and become proficient in their use.

It would be erroneous to say there is a further drift to war. Russia has been warned that such a conflict could well spread, threatening world holocaust; that even if it were limited Western military forces might have to intervene. In such case they would probably retain bases afterward which they do not now possess. Moscow is terrified of Allied bases anywhere. But even if the U.S.S.R. and democratic powers are restudying their positions, the direct participants, Israel and the Arab lands, remain hostile, suspicious and full of hatred. There might not be a further drift to war. But certainly there is no drift to peace.

V. THE UNITED STATES IN THE CHANGING MIDDLE EAST

EDITOR'S INTRODUCTION

In concluding this book with comments on United States policy toward the Middle East no comprehensive discussion is attempted; other articles above have often referred to American policy, its direction, its problems and failures. In addition, it appears that United States policy may be at a point of significant change but only time will make this clear.

The first article here summarizes views held by many in the Middle Eastern lands about United States policies generally. Criticisms within the local area as well as those at home are needed in judging our policies. Following is an official statement covering mainly policy matters on military defense of the area. Next, in turn, a drastic criticism of United States policy and a plea for Anglo-American-French action on the many questions in the Middle East are given. Whether as a matter of policy the American government should sell arms to Israel is debated in the next two selections. Then a short statement is presented on how the basic problem confronting the United States in such regions relates to the arming of Israel. The short editorial points up growing American recognition that, having aided in the establishment of Israel, we must face the price of insuring peace in the area. And last, will United States policy shift? This question is posed by an early reaction to the withdrawal of Western aid in building the Aswan Dam, which resulted in Egypt's retaliation in nationalizing the Suez Canal. This book must end then on an inconclusive note. As the scene in the Middle East continues to shift, we may expect crisis to follow crisis.

HOW MIDDLE EASTERNERS LOOK AT
U. S. POLICY [1]

In the Arab world and the rest of the Middle East, from Gibraltar to India and from the Black Sea down to the Sudan, the United States has unquestionably lost heavily in prestige and friendship in the last few years. In the Arab countries, at least, that trend is continuing.

The reasons given by critics vary but the best simple generalization might be summed up as "too much and too little." The United States has aided nationalist aspirations and fought colonialism enough to annoy and harm its British and French allies and not enough to win the solid friendship of local nationalists.

The Americans have given generously and yet have hesitated enough, made enough conditions and refused enough requests to irritate those who are receiving the gifts and loans.

The phase of United States policy that has won the most favorable comments and made the most friends has been the technical and educational aid that is being so widely given.

Against that, the most criticized factor in United States policy is unquestionably its support of Israel. The Arab world looks on the United States as the principal force in the creation and protection of Israel as a state. When one sees how bitterly the Arabs feel about that, the most surprising point is that there is still so much friendliness for the United States.

Balanced Arab opinion does not hold now that it is possible to do away with Israel. But it does reproach the United States for what the Arabs believe to be a consistently strong bias in favor of Israel as against her Moslem neighbors.

The Israelis, on their side, feel the United States could assure their survival in peace by arming them heavily.

If the United States gave in on that point, there would be extreme alarm on the Arab side and an immediate rush to the Soviet bloc for arms that have been offered and that have been bought on a small scale.

[1] From "Precise U.S. Policy Asked in Mideast," by Sam Pope Brewer, New York *Times* correspondent in the Middle East. New York *Times.* p 1+. April 4, 1956. Reprinted by permission.

The Israelis approve economic aid policies and the plan advanced by Eric Johnston, President Eisenhower's representative, for rational development of Jordan Valley waterpower and irrigation resources.

They think the United States should arm them and keep arms from the Arab countries. They believe the United States puts too much faith in the ability of the United Nations to prevent a major war in the Middle East.

As an improvement on present policies, they urge heavy "defensive" armament for Israel and the use of all possible pressures to impose a settlement of Israel's frontiers that would involve recognition of Israel's existence as a state.

The Arabs oppose such a settlement because they feel their whole position rests on the fact they have never consented to the establishment of a foreign state in an area inhabited by Arabs. Recognition of Israel, they believe, would weaken their claim to the area involved. . . .

In Egypt, the Israeli question is the pivot of the attitude toward the United States. The Egyptians are elated with the success of their revolution. They believe Premier Gamal Abdel Nasser outmaneuvered the United States when he obtained arms from Czechoslovakia.

Now they would be satisfied with no less change in United States policy than complete abandonment of Israel and full support of Premier Nasser's new Egypt in her aspirations to dominate the Arab world.

In common with other Arabs, the Egyptians talk vaguely about the United States refusal to "face realities" but they produce no workable alternative to present American policy.

The Baghdad Pact provides an example of the vacillation that has brought criticism of the United States from all sides.

United States refusal to join has irritated and alarmed the member countries, organized for defense against Soviet aggression. The members, Britain, Iraq, Iran, Pakistan and Turkey, feel that the success or failure of the alliance depends on the active membership or absence of the United States, which first suggested it.

Foes of the pact include the Soviet bloc and "neutralist" countries, with Egypt leading the chorus of criticism. They resent United States moral support of this pact, even though it has not gone beyond lip service.

One senior United States diplomat commented bitterly recently that it was impossible to know where the United States stood as long as it refused to join the pact, although the State Department periodically proclaimed its support of the alliance.

A result is that the United States incurs the ill will of both opposed camps.

The Turks, too, have criticisms of United States policy, but they do not hinge on the Israeli question.

Turkey's objections are connected chiefly with financial questions. They accuse the United States of trying to shape everybody into the American mold. That criticism is heard elsewhere and Americans living abroad generally concede there is some justice in it.

The Turks are in financial difficulties and feel that the United States has been too reluctant to bail them out and unduly critical of some of the conduct that has landed them in that position.

In all these countries, another criticism frequently heard is that the United States focuses all its attention on the fight against communism and opposes even commercial relations with the Soviet Union and its satellites.

They believe the United States exaggerates the Red menace and they suspect mercenary motives behind the objections to their trade with the Soviet bloc.

The forces with which United States policy has to deal in the Arab world, Turkey, Iran and the rest of the Middle East are multiple. Communism is not the most conspicuous.

Nationalism is the most notable force and in these countries has become virtually synonymous with anti-Western sentiment. . . .

The Communists manipulate those nationalist forces. Sometimes the Reds pose as having nationalist aims themselves. Sometimes they convince the nationalists that "after all we have the same enemies—the Western imperialists—and party names do not matter."

Communism as an open political force is not dangerous in most of these countries. The danger lies in the fact that the nationalists think they can cooperate with the Communists as long as it suits them and then drop them. The nationalists overlook the damage done meanwhile.

In Syria, for example, there appears to be strong Communist influence, though the party as such does not amount to much. There is one Communist member of Parliament, Khaled Bagdash, but the greatest danger again lies not in him but in some of the young officers and officials who believe Communist agitation and Communist aid from abroad are useful weapons against the Western powers and who do not realize the danger of falling into the Communists' grip.

In the Arab countries, simple hostility to Israel and fear of her supposed ambitions for expansion may also be classed as a specific force working against the United States. Until after World War II Americans were known in these countries only as benefactors. They had neither colonies nor mandates. They did provide schools and colleges, encourage the Arab political revival and send aid when there were disasters.

That vast fund of good will is not exhausted but it is depleted by the struggle over Israel and because of United States inability to abandon its French and British allies to please the Arab nationalists. . . .

The United States obviously would not gain by plunging recklessly onto one side or the other in each controversy, or by ladling out money without knowing what was being done with it.

There do stand out in the opinions from various countries certain calls for policy changes that seem to occur to many persons of different groups.

The basic one is a plea to decide on some definite policy, whatever it may be. In most cases, this means a demand for a policy backing up the speaker's particular group.

In the instances mentioned above, it is clear the United States cannot well drop its moderate position and back one side fully. But the so-called middle-of-the-road position too often looks like indecision.

The call is for a clear-cut policy. It would still not please the partisan groups but they would have fewer false hopes.

On less general lines, there are clear indications that money put into education facilities, libraries and technical aid is well spent. There are different views about the efficiency of existing operations in that field but there is no doubt about the demand among Middle Eastern peoples for the facilities provided.

That effectiveness is presumably why the United States Information Service library in any city is normally the first target of hoodlums whenever political disturbances start. The Communists invariably seize the chance to steer violence into channels that suit their purpose, and the American library is almost invariably their first objective. . . .

Several observers think policies on loans and grants might be reviewed.

The Soviet Union has been making much headway directly and through satellites in providing underdeveloped countries with things they want, whether they are arms, industrial equipment or other material. They give no gifts but make business deals on terms that amount to the same thing without calling for acknowledgment of that fact. Payment may be in surplus products the aid recipients could not sell elsewhere or in weak currencies and spread over a long period.

The Soviet does not moralize about whether a country should have the arms it seeks or whether it needs the type of factory it wants.

A result is that each deal creates much good will at relatively low cost. Carefully supervised American loans and gifts, however lavish they may be, tend to leave the recipient with the feeling of the tramp who is required to sing a hymn to get a free cup of coffee.

A STATE DEPARTMENT VIEW [2]

[The Middle East] contains great human and physical resources. The population includes some 40 million Arabs, more than 1.5 million Israelis, more than 70 million Pakistanis, and

[2] From "Middle East Defense," by John D. Jernegan, Deputy Assistant Secretary for Near Eastern, South Asian, and African Affairs. *United States Department of State Bulletin.* 32:564-9. April 4, 1955.

about 20 million, each, Iranians and Turks. The vast majority are, of course, Moslems, but these peoples also include important elements adhering to the other two great monotheistic religions, and all of them share in varying degrees a mingled heritage of Eastern and Western culture. Historically, at different times and in different ways, each of the peoples now living in the area has had an important impact on our own Western civilization and has in turn been influenced by the West. Today, each nation and each group of peoples in the area has vitally important relations with nations and peoples outside of the area.

What happens in the Middle East, therefore, cannot be treated as in a vacuum, as an isolated phenomenon. Events in that region have political, economic, psychological, and spiritual repercussions on vast areas of the world. These repercussions are magnified and brought more clearly to the public eye by the existence of the United Nations as a world forum and by the great development in recent years in the means of international communication and the consequent political and economic inter-dependence of all nations and areas. On top of this, we have the strain between the free world and the Communist world, which has produced a situation in which no area of the world can be regarded as unimportant to the security of the United States.

Our country, in addition, has certain special ties with the Middle East—sentimental ties, if you will. We have a tradition of more than a century of philanthropic work in that area. Our scholars have devoted much time and effort to its archeology and history. Nearly the whole of the American people looks to that area as the birthplace of its religions. Many of our citizens have come from the area, and many Americans have strong ties of family or sentiment with the area. Furthermore, the United States as a nation and many of its citizens as individuals have played a role in bringing about the independence of the new nation states which make up a large part of the Middle East. We have, naturally, a keen and sympathetic interest in the maintenance of their independence and in their progress toward greater economic and social well-being.

Resources of Middle East

From the aspect of physical resources, the importance of the Middle East to the United States, and the rest of the world, stands out equally clearly. Its natural resources include some three fifths of the known oil reserves of the whole world. I need hardly underline the significance of this one fact. Western Europe and much of Asia and Africa depend almost entirely on this source of supply. If this oil ceased to be freely available in world markets, whether in peace or in war, the consequences are easy to imagine. This great natural resource is, obviously, of vital importance to the countries where it is produced as well as to those which consume it. The producing nations derive from it great revenues which hold forth a prospect of major economic and social progress for their peoples.

But oil is not the only resource of the Middle East. The area contains others which can be developed for the benefit both of the area and of the consumers of the world. The most valuable resource of all is in the field of agriculture. Great things have already been done to increase productivity and greater things are to come. Industry is also beginning to develop.

Its function as a communications link, alone, would make the Middle East an area of extreme importance. The Suez Canal is the key to the trade route between Europe and Asia, and the areas to the north and east of the Canal form the path for aerial communication between the two continents. . . .

This area is one whose loss to the free world would be a major disaster. Yet, unless we do something, it is quite possible that this loss will take place.

Traditionally, the Middle East has been an object of Russian ambition. This was true under the Czars, and it has continued to be true under the Soviet regime. It is more than ever true today. Until some eight or nine years ago, the Russian drive to the south was contained primarily by the existence of British strength in South Asia and the Near East. Since World War II the basis of British power in this region has been greatly reduced. Britain has withdrawn from the Indian subcontinent and from

Palestine, and she is in the process of withdrawing from Egypt. From the long-range political point of view, this withdrawal was undoubtedly wise and necessary. It has recognized the legitimate political development and aspirations of the peoples concerned and has left them free to pursue their aspirations in their own way, but it has also left them largely defenseless against expansion by a predatory great power. There has been, for some two centuries, little or no indigenous defensive strength in the Middle East. Today, that situation still prevails in general despite the elements of strength represented by Turkey and Pakistan and by the small beginnings toward development of such strength in certain other countries. Israel's military strength is already a significant element in the picture.

The United States, conscious of its new responsibilities in the world, has been trying to remedy the weakness of the area. We cannot, and should not, do it in the ways which were customary in the nineteenth century. Even if our own traditions would permit it, the world has changed too much to make the conquest of foreign lands and the establishment of our forces upon them in defiance of the wishes of their inhabitants a practicable procedure. We have been trying instead to cooperate freely and equally, and on a basis of sympathetic impartiality, with the nations most directly concerned. We began with diplomatic support, both within and outside the United Nations. The outstanding example was furnished by Soviet Russia's attempt to take over Iranian Azerbaijan in 1945 and 1946. The United States, as well as the United Nations, can take considerable credit for the failure of that attempt. Another instance is furnished by the Soviet demands upon Turkey in 1945 and 1946 regarding the Black Sea straits and the Kars-Ardahan area of eastern Turkey. We stood firmly behind Turkey's resistance to these demands. But we soon found that diplomatic support was not enough, and we launched our economic and military aid programs in Greece and Turkey in 1947.

These programs, and others which came later, have contributed greatly to the capacity of the Middle East to resist aggressive pressures. They were followed by the adherence of

Greece and Turkey to the North Atlantic Treaty, with the result that a firm barrier was established against invasion of the Middle East from its northwestern corner. Unfortunately, this still does not meet the need. Defensive strength is needed to the east, and it is also essential to have support to the south in order to provide defense in depth. Recognition of this led the United States and its Western associates to seek in 1951 and 1952 the creation of a "Middle East Command" or a "Middle East Defense Organization." These proposals would have grouped Middle Eastern States in a defensive arrangement with the United States, the United Kingdom, France, Turkey, and certain British dominions. They failed of acceptance because the Middle Eastern states were too preoccupied by their local quarrels and by certain then existing disputes with the West to be willing to join in a general defensive arrangement under Western leadership.

Policy of United States

In 1953 Secretary of State Dulles visited the Middle East. He came to two conclusions: first, that most of the Middle Eastern States were unwilling as yet to associate themselves closely with the West in matters of defense; and second, that any sound organization for defense should spring from the desires of the peoples and governments of the area itself. He further found that certain states, in the main those to the north and east, which were closest to the source of potential danger and therefore most exposed, were most aware of the menace, most likely to do something about it, and also so situated as to provide the greatest measure of protection to the area as a whole. These states included Turkey, Iran, Iraq, and Pakistan. Secretary Dulles laid down the policy that the United States should help to strengthen the interrelated defenses of those countries which want strength, not as against each other but to resist the common threat to all free peoples, including the United States. This remains the policy of the American Government.

What we hope therefore is, first, that all the states immediately concerned will come to recognize that they are in danger from a common source and that this overriding danger arises not from local attacks by their neighbors in the area but from a much greater threat which hangs over them as well as the rest of the non-Communist world. Secondly, we hope for a realization that the first step in meeting this threat should be cooperation among themselves for collective defense. We in this country have long been convinced that such cooperation is the only means of insuring ourselves and our friends against engulfment, but we cannot impose this belief on others nor can we force others into collective arrangements. They must themselves arrive at the same belief.

As they do arrive at this belief, we stand ready to encourage their own efforts at cooperation among themselves and to help in developing the strength they will need to make their cooperation most effective.

Progress Toward Collective Defense

I have already referred to what has been accomplished by Greece and Turkey. More recently, highly significant and encouraging beginnings have been made in the process of extending the framework of collective defense to other parts of the Middle East. Last year, Turkey and Pakistan signed, on their own initiative, a treaty which provided for cooperation between the two countries to promote their mutual security. This was followed by the conclusion of a military aid agreement between the United States and Pakistan, which in a sense complemented the already existing military aid arrangements between the United States and Turkey. A little later, Iraq manifested its growing recognition of the need for area security by concluding a similar military aid agreement with the United States. Most recently, on February 24, 1955, Turkey and Iraq signed a treaty of cooperation for mutual defense. Both the Turk-Pakistani and Turk-Iraqi pacts are open to the adherence of other like-minded states. [See "A Pact for the 'Northern Tier,' " in Section I, above.]

In the meantime, some of the disputes between Middle Eastern states and Western states have been resolved. In particular, Britain and Egypt have reached agreement on the long-standing question of the Suez Canal base [though not on the questions of control and use of the Canal—Ed.] Iran, Britain, and the United States have successfully worked out a solution to the Iranian oil problem. This has opened the way to further expansion of cooperative security arrangements. Although they are not yet in agreement as to the form it should take, I think most of the Middle Eastern states are coming to feel the necessity for cooperation and that in due course they will associate themselves in one way or another with realistic and effective arrangements for the defense of the area. The American Government will put no pressure upon them. We prefer that they take their own time and make their own decisions.

You will note that the concept of an area defensive arrangement in the Middle East is still little more than a concept. The new links between Turkey and Iraq and Turkey and Pakistan are still rather vague and general; their operating mechanisms are yet to be created. Also, they are still bilaterial rather than regional arrangements. The existing treaties between Britain on the one hand and Iraq, Jordan, Libya, and Egypt are likewise bilateral. American military assistance agreements are in effect only with Turkey, Iran, Iraq, and Pakistan. Neither party is committed by these aid agreements to any military obligations other than the very general ones of refraining from aggression and of being prepared to assist in its own defense and the defense of the free world. Pakistan, of course, is a member of the Manila Pact, just as Turkey is a member of NATO, but these arrangements are directed toward objectives other than the collective defense of the Middle East.

I make this point to emphasize the distance that has still to be traveled before the Middle East can be said to have a defense organization. I also make it to reassure those who fear that the United States is going too far too fast in building up military defenses in an area which has still to achieve political and economic stability. We have not really gone very far, nor are we, even now, moving very fast.

Lack of Unanimity

It is inherent in the nature of any development of this kind that it must move slowly, especially at first. A whole range of problems must be taken into account. These include, first and foremost, the political attitudes of the countries concerned, but they also include their economic situation, their existing and potential military strength, and the resources which the United States and its associates could muster in support. I can assure you that the American Government takes all these considerations fully into account. We are well aware, as I have already pointed out, that there is as yet no unanimity among the states of the Middle East with regard to the nature of the danger they face and the steps needed to meet the danger. We are well aware, too, that military strength alone is not the answer to their problems, not even the problem of area defense.

They need economic and technical assistance, which we and others are providing and intend to continue to provide. But progress, in our judgment, is being made. Political thought in the area is evolving, by and large, in the direction which we consider sound, and the foundations have been laid, in most cases, for the construction of sound economies. We do not believe we can afford to wait for the solution of all political, economic, and social problems before we look ahead toward a solution of the defense problem. The world situation does not allow such delay. Furthermore, we are convinced that the development of indigenous defensive strength will itself contribute to the solution of political problems. It will give the peoples of the area greater self-confidence as well as greater willingness and ability to cooperate in the collective defense of the area.

Let me repeat that what we are doing is being done with our eyes and minds wide open. We are conscious of the strong tensions which exist between the Arab states and Israel. We also know that there are disputes and divergencies of view among other states of the area, even among the Arab states themselves. The reaction of some Arab states to the conclusion of the recent Turk-Iraqi pact has been one evidence of this. We are therefore being extremely careful that the contributions we make to the military strength of the area go to states which sincerely intend to use them for the purpose of *defending* themselves and their neighbors *against* aggression and not for any aggressive purposes of their own. We insist and intend to insist on guarantees to this effect, in accordance with the terms of our mutual security legislation.

This legislation requires, among other things, that military assistance—

shall be made available solely to maintain the internal security and legitimate self-defense of the recipient nation, or to permit it to participate in the defense of its area or in collective security arrangements and measures consistent with the Charter of the United Nations. The President shall be satisfied that such equipment and materials will not be used to undertake any act of aggression against any nation. . . .

In connection with the military aid agreement with Pakistan, President Eisenhower said:

These undertakings afford adequate assurance to all nations, regardless of their political orientation and whatever their international policies may be, that the arms the United States provides for the defense of the free world will in no way threaten their own security. I can say . . . that if our aid to any country, including Pakistan, is misused and directed against another in aggression I will undertake immediately, in accordance with my constitutional authority, appropriate action both within and without the UN to thwart such aggression.

We also believe that the association of Middle Eastern states with each other in bilateral or multilateral defense arrangements directed against aggression from outside the area is, in itself, a safeguard against their involvement in aggressive moves inside the area. Their very willingness to enter into such agreements is an indication that their attention is directed in the right direction, and their association with other states which are more concerned with the world problem than with intra-area disputes is bound to exercise an influence which can only be beneficial from the point of view of area peace and stability.

It is in this framework, primarily in the context of collective defense arrangements, that we intend to provide military assistance where needed to promote the development of sound plans for area defense.

Special Problem of Israel

What I have said so far applies more or less generally to the whole area. It would be unrealistic to pretend, however, that the state of Israel does not constitute something of a special factor and a special problem in the development of Middle East defense. Let us look frankly at the facts. They are very clear. On the one hand, in the past year or so the government of Israel has made plain its willingness and desire to align itself with the West and to cooperate for the defense of the Middle East against outside aggression. Furthermore, Israel has military forces which could contribute to a considerable degree to the defense of the area. Looking at these two facts alone, it would seem highly logical that Israel should be incorporated in a collective defense arrangement at an early date. But there are other facts that must be considered. Much as we deplore it, we must admit that the relations between Israel and her neighbors are anything but good. They vary from time to time from a state of quiescent hostility to a condition almost of open warfare. So long as such circumstances prevail, there are lacking the necessary foundations for political cooperation between Israel and those states with which her defense must be linked in the long run. In the absence of political cooperation it is, of course, out of the question to make plans involving military cooperation between Israeli forces and those of her immediate neighbors.

I hope I need not tell you that the American Government is gravely concerned at the existence of this state of affairs. We are always concerned at the existence of conflict anywhere in the world, and we especially regret it in an area such as this, where it constitutes a barrier to the proper organization of collective defense. The desire and the hope of reducing tensions between Israel and her neighbors is never out of our minds. We understand the anxiety felt by the people and the government of Israel at their continued isolation in the area of which they are a part. We are doing our best to improve relations. It must be realized that this is complicated by the fact that Israel's neighbors are themselves afraid of aggression on the part of Israel. Every act of violence across the frontiers is a setback to progress. The problem is difficult, but I am confident a solution can be found in time.

I should like to say here that in my opinion Israel as a nation is not in danger, except to the extent that all other states in the Near East are in danger from the common threat of outside aggression. Israel is in fact in less danger than some others of those states. She is not directly in the path of possible Soviet aggression, as are those states which Secretary Dulles has called the "northern tier." I have already mentioned that Israel's armed forces would be capable of contributing to area defense against an aggressive great power. Those forces are still more capable of protecting her against a lesser attack. Relative to others in the region, the Israeli military establishment is highly developed, and it enjoys the advantage of holding interior lines.

What is even more important, I do not see evidence of any intent on the part of her neighbors to attack Israel.

In my view, all this means that we can and should move forward slowly but steadily toward the goal of general Middle East defense, taking one step at a time and avoiding hasty action which would weaken or bring down, before it is fairly begun, the structure which we hope to see created.

We should continue to let the nations of the Middle East take the lead in establishing their own cooperative arrangements. We cannot profitably push any one or more of them into arrangements which they dislike. We can, however, seek to help them along the paths they may choose when those run in a direction we consider helpful to our mutual security, and we can help to fill gaps which may appear in the defense framework as it evolves.

There are many possible forms which a Middle East defense arrangement could take. It might be a single structure, or it might consist of two or more separate but related units. It might be restricted entirely to states in the area itself, assisted and supported in some fashion by states outside the area, or it might include among its members those Western states which have the desire and ability to work directly for the defense of the area.

It is too early to make sound forecasts as to the character which organization for collective defense in this region may assume. Nevertheless, I think it is safe to predict that the concept of collective defense will take material shape in the not-too-distant future and that this will redound to the benefit of all the states in the Middle East as well as the United States.

A CRITICISM OF U. S. POLICY [3]

Whether the loss of China to the Communists could have been prevented by a wiser American policy is doubtful but perhaps debatable.

If, on the other hand, the Middle East is lost to Soviet influence, there will be no question that this catastrophe could have been prevented. The fault will lie in the first instance at the door of stubborn Anglo-French colonialism, but to a very large extent the responsibility will be shared by the United States, and chiefly by the Eisenhower Administration.

Our postwar diplomacy has consistently underestimated the extent to which British power was diminished by the last war.

A true appraisal would have dictated one of two courses in the Mediterranean area: to step into the vacuum, as we did in Greece; or to persuade both the British in the Middle East and the French in North Africa that the only sensible course for them to pursue would be to withdraw gracefully and in time, as the British did in India.

We adopted neither of these alternatives. We intervened in Greece because there was a direct Communist threat—the only sort of threat to which our postwar diplomacy has been sensitive.

In the Middle East and North Africa there was no Communist threat but a rising revolt against Western domination and exploitation. With respect to this we took an ambivalent attitude.

By our half-hearted backing of Anglo-French colonialism we alienated most of the peoples of Asia and the Arab world; by our

[3] From a letter to the *Times,* "Middle East Reexamined," by James P. Warburg, writer on foreign affairs. New York *Times.* p9. March 18, 1956. Reprinted by permission.

failure to make our support of colonialism at least effective we merely encouraged our two major allies to pursue a course foredoomed to failure.

In addition, our only positive policy in this area—support of the creation of a Jewish state—complicated matters further because we failed to see to it that the Arab-Israeli war ended in a just peace settlement, both as to frontiers and as to the care and resettlement of the Arabs displaced from Palestine.

The Middle East legacy left by the Truman Administration was bad enough, but it remained for the Eisenhower Administration to convert a precarious situation into outright disaster. Obsessed by the notion of encircling the Communist orbit with military alliances and in flagrant disregard of the political tensions existing in the area, Secretary of State Dulles sponsored the rearmament of the Arab states. The result of this effort was to open the whole area to Communist political penetration without creating even the semblance of a barrier to military invasion.

Egypt and Saudi Arabia have now become the core of a growing Arab-Asian neutralism as between the Communist and anti-Communist forces, as well as the focal point of an anti-colonial revolt which has spread into North Africa. At the same time the rearming of the Arab states has created renewed tensions with Israel and the likelihood of war. One of our two most important allies now faces the loss of its major source of oil and hard currency. The other faces the loss of its African empire, without which it will sink to the rank of a third-rate power.

The consequences of this disaster are not confined to the Middle East and North Africa. NATO is the core of the anti-Communist defense alignment. Because of the Middle East fiasco NATO's southern flank has disintegrated. (Greece is disaffected; the quarrel over Cyprus has ruptured the Greco-Turkish alliance; Yugoslavia is drifting toward the neutralist Arab-Asian bloc.) Worse yet, NATO has been dangerously weakened at its vital center by the withdrawal to North Africa of the cream of its French contingents.

The Democrats have a far stronger case against the Republicans with respect to the Middle East than the Republicans had against them over China in 1952. But by exploiting the

Republican failure the Democrats will render both themselves and the nation a service only if they come forward with a constructive alternative.

Such an alternative must recognize not only the need for massive economic assistance but also that it is now too late for any patchwork of appeasement.

It must seek to come to terms not only with Arab and Israeli nationalism but with that extraneous power which our own folly has now made a factor throughout the area.

A PLEA FOR JOINT ANGLO-AMERICAN-FRENCH POLICY [4]

In Britain we are so desperately concerned with the absence of mutual cooperation between Britain and America in our Middle East policy that I write this letter.

The threat of war in the Middle East is imminent. If the present policy continues, the mutual interests of Britain and America will be undermined and our oil and other interests endangered. If there is indecision and evasion and a failure to achieve effective joint decisions in this era throughout election year it will have tragic and permanent effects on the course of world history. The only beneficiary from such indecision will be communism.

The present trend of events in the Middle East show clearly that Colonel Nasser as military dictator of Egypt has sworn to get us out of the Middle East, and has pledged himself to destroy our association with friendly Arab nations, whose alliance with us is being undermined by Saudi-Arabian gold. This policy, designed to eradicate all Western influence throughout the Arab world, includes both France and America.

The aim of Colonel Nasser is to form a federation of Arab states, of which he would become the head. He is using the Arab hatred of Israel to weld the states together into an effective

[4] From a letter to the *Times*, "For a Middle East Policy," by W. R. Rees-Davies, Member of the British House of Commons. New York *Times*. p 30. April 17, 1956. Reprinted by permission.

instrument. If Nasser succeeds in his purpose Egypt could thereby secure effective control of the vast oil resources of the Middle East.

The Goebbellesque methods which he employs of the continuous incitement to violence through the press and the Cairo radio, although they are the time-honored weapons of military dictatorship, are being successfully directed.

At present we have the bitter irony of the position in which American gold, filling the coffers of Saudi Arabia, is being used by the Arabs in the name of Arab unity to foster hatred against Britain and France.

Another instance can be briefly stated with regard to Jordan—where the Communists, who twelve months ago had no influence, have now become the most powerful faction.

Without Western influence and Western economic aid Egypt with her few resources is driven into the arms of Russia for economic support—hence the recent supply of arms by the Communists to Egypt.

There is an immediate need for a joint policy in the Middle East between the Tripartite powers—America, Britain and France —before the situation further deteriorates.

First we need an emphatic joint statement by our respective governments of our adherence to the terms of the Tripartite Declaration, made in May 1950, of our "unalterable opposition to the use of force or threat of force between any of the states in that area," and a restatement that we shall "immediately take action, both within and outside the United Nations to prevent" such use of force or threat of force.

Secondly, a joint declaration that the three powers have evolved methods of determining who is the aggressor and will exercise their duty to intervene and to prevent war.

Thirdly, industrial action is vital. The leaders of the oil industry, both in America and Britain, should meet immediately to formulate a common policy, designed to maintain our mutual spheres of influence and to insure that the industry does not take any action through lack of understanding which will damage our mutual interests.

Finally, the Arabs, who have always been friendly in the past to the Western powers, must be made to realize that their future prosperity depends upon our economic aid and our economic skill and assistance, which is at their service. The loss of our mutual influence in the Middle East would be no less a tragedy to the underdeveloped Arab states than to the Western powers.

If we are forced to get out of the Middle East, communism will fill the vacuum.

NEEDED: ARMS TO ISRAEL [5]

The armistice border between Israel and the Arab states has become not only the newest but the most active Communist front in the whole world. Here we see the new Communist power thrust—post-Geneva style.

The "summit" conference at Geneva marked one of the turning points in world history. For there the United States seized the peace initiative away from the Communists. We have yet to fully exploit this advantage, but we did seize the initiative. Our challenge was very puzzling to the Communists, and they are now trying to answer it by vaulting right into the center of the Middle East, an area in which communism had not been so active in recent years.

This maneuver presents for us totally new problems in world politics. Here is a Communist effort to win peoples not by force and propaganda alone but also by economic and military assistance, hitherto our specialty. On the Israel-Arab issue the Communists have exploited the intransigence of the Arabs for their own purposes, in an effort to use it as a reason for, and the basis of, their infiltration and ultimate penetration of the whole Middle East area. They are exploiting the fact that many Arab leaders seem to have little constructive hope to offer their people and, instead, offer them hatred of Israel. The Communists are arming the Arabs and proffering them economic and technical assistance for the sake of fomenting and bringing on an Arab-

[5] From "Should the U.S. Sell Arms to Israel?" article by Jacob K. Javits, former member of the House of Representatives (Republican, New York), now Attorney General of New York State and 1956 candidate for the United States Senate. *Foreign Policy Bulletin*. 35:84+. February 15, 1956. Reprinted by permission.

Israeli struggle, which they wish to regard as inevitable. They believe that in this struggle, no matter who wins or who loses, communism can gain the most.

The United States faces a situation where Israeli-Arab tension is not merely an isolated factor within an isolated area of the world, but creates the likelihood of a conflict of the utmost moment to our policy in its most vital aspects. This is the new issue we face in the latest phase of the struggle between freedom and communism.

For Israel, this is a fight for survival. The people of Israel are not foolish. They have tremendous confidence in their own courage and in the indomitable will of their small country. But they know that the life of their new nation could be extinguished just like that—by one little decision—a decision which, I might say without rancor, the British came pretty close to making on November 9, 1955, when Sir Anthony Eden, Britain's prime minister, in his Guildhall speech suggested the reduction of Israel's territory by 30 per cent. For if one would destroy Israel without a shot the best way to extinguish its hopes for the future is to cut it off from the Negev. And that is the proposal which Prime Minister Eden in effect suggested.

In this struggle there is yet another factor—that of time. It would be good if we had time to work out this problem carefully and deliberately. But the Israelis told me—and I think this is a reasonable estimate—that the arms furnished by the Communists to Egypt, and through Egypt to Syria and Saudi Arabia, are so overwhelming in terms of military superiority that even if inadequately handled they would still represent a decisive advantage in war. . . .

The point is that, valorous and heroic as the Israelis are, they cannot defeat jet aircraft, even badly operated, with traditional or orthodox-type aircraft, even if expertly run. And this is true right down the line about other weapons.

What, under these circumstances, does Israel need?

First, Israel urgently needs a commitment of arms for "legitimate self-defense," in the words of President Eisenhower— strictly scrutinized to be just that. The Israelis themselves invite such scrutiny.

I emphasize the word arms "commitment" because arms cannot be delivered overnight.

Second, Israel needs to be included in some form of regional security arrangements or in a direct mutual defense agreement with the United States, modeled on our mutual defense agreements with the Republic of China on Formosa, with Japan and with the Philippines. Israel needs to have this same kind of security pledge.

But arms for legitimate self-defense are needed, too. There is in effect a three-power declaration of May 1950, made by the United States, Britain and France, which guarantees the inviolability of the armistice borders between Israel and the Arab states. But, say the Israelis, it may take a week, two weeks, a month or two months to actually implement that guarantee by military force if need be, and in that time "we could," they say, "be extinguished as a people, considering the size and strategic vulnerability of our country," so that even this existing guarantee is not adequate for their dangerous situation.

Besides, why ask the people of the United States to risk another case of Communist-fomented armed aggression, Korea style, when the people of Israel are ready to fight in their own defense against such aggression if allowed to acquire the necessary arms with which to defend themselves?

Our country, as I see it, cannot allow war to break out in the Middle East, nor can we allow the Communists to capture the Middle East.

And so our government needs to make a decision, and make it promptly. Perhaps the most urgent matter in American policy today—based on my observation of the situation in Israel— is the need for prompt decision. I can see no real alternative to a decision that would reassure Israel regarding its independence and security by arms, strictly limited to legitimate self-defense—in the first instance. Only in this way can the path to Arab-Israeli peace across the bridge of regional economic and social interest again be opened. I believe there can be no other conclusion because the alternative is either surrender to the Communists or appeasement. Should we allow the Communists to show the Arab states how to liquidate Israel, we will have guaranteed a vast increase in Communist prestige in the Middle East, and perhaps even the creation of new Communist satellites there. And yield we never will; appeasement, as we have learned since Munich, is only the first step before admitting defeat.

All this presents a serious situation to the people of our country.

When we get into extremely complex and difficult political situations internationally, when there is a tremendous conflict of interests or when there are very complex considerations on one side and the other, our country has inevitably made a moral decision.

It would be an act unworthy of our country to allow Israel to go down the drain.

Hence, we should decide for saving Israel in our national interest because it is the moral decision. And so, let us do it in time—fully, deliberately and effectively.

NO ARMS FOR ISRAEL [6]

The United States should not sell arms to Israel.

The danger of an all-out Arab-Israeli war has been growing at an alarming rate in the past six months. Zionist and other pro-Israeli groups have been urging the Eisenhower Administration to sell arms to Israel, in order to offset the Czech arms recently sold to Egypt.

Such a move would step up the arms race—which has been going on quietly but unrelentingly since 1948—by encouraging the Soviet bloc to make further sales to the Arab states. It would destroy what remains of Arab faith in American fair play. It would disastrously weaken the internal position of moderate Arab leaders, who are the West's chief hope for a peaceful settlement. Instead of halting the drift toward war, even a "token" sale of American weapons to Israel would carry any peaceful settlement beyond the realm of practical politics.

[6] From "Should U.S. Sell Arms to Israel?" by Mather Eliot, Middle East Director of American Friends of the Middle East at Damascus, Syria. *Foreign Policy Bulletin*. 35:85-6. February 15, 1956. Reprinted by permission.

Only a drastic change of American policy—coordinated with Britain, France and, if possible, Russia—offers a reasonable chance of preventing war. We must act, and act fast, if this chance is to be seized.

"Sympathetic impartiality" has been the keynote of the Eisenhower-Dulles policy. To date, this policy has not succeeded because it has not been implemented. What the Administration has offered are the palliative proposals of the Johnston plan for joint Israeli-Arab use of the Jordan waters and Mr. Dulles' Council on Foreign Relations speech of August 26 [1955, offering money and assistance to end the dispute]. Neither the Arabs nor the Israelis have accepted either proposal. Popular passions, instead of subsiding, have risen higher. Border incidents have multiplied.

The causes of the conflict lie deeper.

For eight years the Israelis, without offering significant concessions, have pleaded for peace. In these eight years the Arabs have steadfastly refused to make peace except on the basis of the UN resolutions of 1947-1948, which would require Israel to give up the territory gained by conquest in the fighting of 1947-1948.

Arab stubbornness results from a deeply felt sense of injustice. In international conflicts justice never is wholly with one side. But in this particular conflict American policy-makers must take into account the fact that the balance of justice is on the Arab side. To ask a man to permit, without resistance, the destruction of his country is to ask him to commit a kind of suicide.

The tragedy is that the creation of the state of Israel resulted in the destruction of Arab Palestine and made 800,000 Palestinian Arabs homeless. It was inevitable that in the course of time the 42 million Arabs in the Middle East would rally in support of their Palestinian brothers.

Peace in Palestine is not possible through a compromise worked out on the present position of the contending sides, as Mr. Dulles proposed in his speech before the Council on Foreign Relations. A deeper compromise is necessary, taking into account the whole evolution of events since the Balfour Declaration of 1917. It is a compromise between the 80 per cent of original Arab Palestine which the Arabs lost to Israel in this period, and the whole of what the Zionists have gained in thirty-nine years of effort—effort which succeeded only because the Arabs were too weak to resist successfully.

I believe the Arabs will accept this compromise now, but no other. They will take half a loaf now for the sake of peace, but they will continue to resist if they are offered what to them is no bread at all. And time is on their side. In another year or two the rising tide of Arab bitterness, buttressed by the U.S.S.R. as well as by the Arabs' own rapidly growing economic and military strength, will make even this compromise impossible.

There is no evidence that the present leaders of Israel are prepared to make any such compromise. This, too, is understandable. No country, and especially not one including European Jews who suffered under Hitler, would find it easy to relinquish territory. It is difficult indeed in the light of present circumstances for Israeli leaders to appreciate where their own long-range interests really lie.

Such an impasse cannot be allowed to continue. It provides too good an opportunity for the U.S.S.R. to swing another entire bloc of nations into its camp.

To be specific, the settlement of the Arab-Israeli conflict which is still practicable would have to contain at least three elements:

1. American pressure upon Israel to accept the UN resolutions of 1947-1948 as the point of departure for new negotiations. The settlement to be expected from such negotiations is that Israel would relinquish about 20 per cent of its present territory, including northern Galilee and the southern half of the Negev. This would permit approximately 300,000 Arab refugees to return to their original homes.

2. American financial aid to compensate and help resettle both the 500,000 Palestinian Arabs who do not return to their original homes and the Israeli Jews who will be displaced from their present homes in the areas ceded by Israel.

3. An international guarantee of the new Israeli frontiers, through the United Nations.

This settlement is squarely based on America's national and global interests. It is as fair a settlement, both to Arabs and Israelis, as the facts will now permit. Moreover, it is a settlement in accord with rapidly crystallizing world opinion.

Until very recently the Arab-Israeli dispute was virtually ignored by three fourths of mankind. But all this changed last spring when the Bandung conference endorsed the Arabs' basic contention that the UN resolutions of 1947-1948 must be enforced. Bandung was the turning point. Now the U.S.S.R., and Yugoslavia as well, have followed suit. This leaves the United States and Britain no real choice. The middle world— Indonesia, India, Iran, Turkey, Tito, and their associates—have said very clearly where they believe justice lies. Either we go along or we give the game up to Russia. For in this instance the neutrals and all the small nations of the middle world have right on their side. It is the United States and Britain, pressured by Zionism, who have erred all along.

The question may be asked, What assurance can one give that the Arabs, having taken 20 per cent of Israel's territory, will then be satisfied? Will this not whet their appetite for more, until they destroy the whole of Israel?

To this there is a valid answer. My proposal is that Israel's new frontiers should be internationally guaranteed through the United Nations. The negotiations leading to the determination of these frontiers need not be concluded until the Arab states themselves agree to participate in the guarantee, along with India and the rest of what I have called the middle world. On these terms United States and British armed forces, in the last resort, could safely be used to protect Israel. But there would be no last resort because world opinion would then swing to Israel's side. Then the U.S.S.R. and Arab extremists would be cornered and would have to give in. Now it is Israel—with the United States and Britain—which are about to be cornered and forced to yield or to fight.

THE BASIC PROBLEM [7]

One of the great unsolved problems of the modern world [was described by] Chip Bohlen, the American Ambassador in the Soviet Union, . . . years ago:

Everybody talks about the blunders of Yalta, he said, but our greatest blunder has been our tendency to underestimate the revolutionary effects of the last great war on British power, and our failure to act quickly and effectively to fill the vacuum.

The roots of this problem run back hundreds of years and involve not only the aspirations of former colonial peoples but fierce religious conflicts. Consequently, it will take a long time to create a new system of security to replace the old colonial system. But there are immediate problems of an alarming nature which must be dealt with in a hurry.

For example, it is widely assumed that by refusing to sell arms to Israel the United States has minimized the danger of getting involved with its own troops in that area. As a matter of fact, the opposite is the case.

Instead of selling these arms and thus placing primary responsibility on Israel for its own defense, the United States has refused and told the Israelis to rely for their defense on the United Nations—which, as we saw in Korea, means primarily the United States—and on the United States-British-French declaration of May 25, 1950.

This declaration stated the "unalterable opposition" of the United States to the use or threat of force by the Arabs or the Israelis in that area and committed the United States to take action "immediately" to prevent any violation of the frontiers or armistice lines.

To the credit of the Eisenhower Administration it has not played politics with this question, which is more than can be said for its Democratic predecessors. But the President is not in a position to take action "immediately" if war should break out, for he has not submitted the question of the 1950 declaration to the Congress.

[7] From "A Dangerous Oversight in American Policy," by James Reston, chief of the New York *Times* Washington Bureau. New York *Times*. p E 10. March 11, 1956.

With American ships already in the area, and the whole region in turmoil, this is a serious oversight. Lacking congressional support the President's declaration places a moral obligation on the United States but leaves doubt in the minds of the antagonists about what the United States would do in the event of war, and how fast it would act.

Similarly, without congressional sanction, there is always the possibility that this country could get involved in a war between Arabs and Jews under conditions which could easily split the Congress, inflame the nation, and leave the President in a more embarrassing position than Mr. Truman on Korea.

This is not to suggest that we have come to another brink. On the contrary, there is considerable evidence that the hotheads on both sides are losing influence rather than gaining it. Nevertheless, the situation is unpredictable. Revolutionary zeal and violence have a way of spreading, and the constitutional problem can be remedied without adding to United States commitments: by seeking congressional approval to take whatever military action the President deems necessary to maintain peace, as was done in the case of Formosa.

Meanwhile, the deeper problem remains and cries for the kind of steady, consistent reappraisal that has not been seen here in months.

The Pax Britannica of the nineteenth century has collapsed. The Communists have moved with speed and cunning to exploit it. And the American Government . . . is trying to "muddle through"—which is what contributed to the collapse of Pax Britannica in the first place.

FACING THE PRICE [8]

President Eisenhower and Prime Minister Sir Anthony Eden [meeting in Washington in early February 1956] took a hard look at the explosive situation in the Middle East. They reached the conclusion, rightly we believe, that the "most urgent need"

[8] From an editorial, "For Peace in the Middle East." *Business Week.* p 176. February 11, 1956. Reprinted by permission.

today is an Arab-Israel settlement. And they called on both sides to "reconcile the positions which they have hitherto taken."

As we see it, this badly needed process of pacification will get nowhere unless there is an end to the Arab-Israel arms race. American politicians, be they Democrats or Republicans, who urge more arms for Israel are not contributing to a relaxation of tension in the Middle East—or to the security of Israel.

It is said that the Soviet arms deal with Egypt has put a new complexion on this conflict, that we must help redress the balance in Israel's favor. This strikes us as the most dangerous kind of reasoning. Whatever Moscow's game is, and it is safe to assume the worst, there is this much to be said for Premier Nasser of Egypt: He made this deal only after (1) an unexpected Israeli attack late in February 1955; and (2) an unsuccessful effort to get arms from the United States.

But the real point is this: Israel cannot hope to find security by trying to maintain its present military superiority over its Arab neighbors. With some 1.7 million Israelis pitted against more than 40 million Arabs, there can be no doubt about which side has the greater long-run capacity to absorb arms. There can be no doubt, either, that more United States arms for Israel today mean more Soviet arms for Egypt tomorrow—probably on a two- or three-to-one basis. In this kind of race neither Israel nor the United States can win.

What we must do in this situation is to find a formula on which enduring peace can be built. There are two key problems—establishing recognized borders for Israel and taking care of the 800,000 displaced Arabs who now are in refugee camps. Our proposals to meet these problems must bear the stamp of equity before world opinion. Then we must try to persuade both the Arab nations and Israel to accept them as a basis for negotiation. Meanwhile we will have to be prepared, as Eisenhower and Eden warned, to intervene with force if either side uses force to violate the present frontier and armistice lines.

There is no way the United States can escape its responsibility in this situation. Without our support the state of Israel would not have been born. Without money from here it could not have lived. That means we are morally committed to see that the state of Israel survives.

But we cannot forget the Arab side of the equation. In Arab eyes the creation of Israel was nothing less than an imperialist invasion, which they were forced to accept because of Western strength.

For years now the American people have been playing the ostrich in this situation, refusing to face the fact that some day we would have to pay a price for having changed the balance of power in a strategic area.

Peace in the Middle East, and Israel's security, depend on our ability to face this fact.

WILL U. S. POLICY SHIFT? [9]

By deciding . . . [in late July 1956] not to help Egypt build the High Dam at Aswan on the Nile, the Administration put an abrupt end to its protracted efforts to win the favor of Premier Gamal Abdel Nasser of Egypt.

In effect, the Administration said to the Soviet Union: "We don't like this deal. You can have it if you want it."

This was not meant to signify that the United States was abandoning the Middle East to the Russians or turning against the Arabs generally. It did, however, mark the end of one important episode in this Administration's foreign policy and the beginning of another, the ultimate significance of which can only be guessed. . . .

[When] Mr. Dulles concluded on . . . [his trip to the Middle East that] Egypt would not join a Western defense alliance, . . . he began working for the "northern tier of defense," later the Baghdad Pact, as an alternative.

Although Egypt indignantly opposed the northern tier idea, the Administration went right on cultivating the Egyptians. It wanted to offset what it considered the Truman Administration's

[9] From "Aswan Decision Marks a Turn in U.S. Policy," by Dana Adams Schmidt, New York *Times* Washington correspondent. New York *Times*. p E3. July 22, 1956. Reprinted by permission.

overt pro-Israeli line. It thought that a friendlier, stronger Egypt might lead the Arab world, if not into a defensive organization, at least into peace with Israel.

The Administration saw to it that Egypt for the first time got development assistance, at the rate of about $40 million a year.

It urged the British at last to give in to Egypt's demand that Britain give up the Suez Canal zone. And the British yielded.

A little more than a year ago the Administration named as Ambassador to Cairo Colonel Henry A. Byroade, who had gained a reputation as friend of the Arabs and as a critic of the Israelis.

But all this was in vain. Mr. Byroade got off to a bad start when the Egyptian Government decided to barter cotton for arms from Communist Czechoslovakia rather than strip its treasury to pay hard cash for United States arms.

Then came the High Dam affair. The World Bank had been studying it for several years and was convinced of its technical feasibility. The weak point was Egypt. Could she stand the internal costs of a $1.3 billion project for which she would have to provide about $900 million in internal costs over a twelve-to-eighteen-year period?

This would require many years of economic austerity if inflation and runaway costs were to be avoided. In spite of official Egyptian assurances, very few of the American and World Bank officials concerned were convinced that the Nasser regime, with its great ambitions, would be capable of such austerity.

It is safe to assume, therefore, that international politics—the conviction that this should be a Western job and that it would be dangerous to let the Russians do it—played a big part in the United States and British decision last December, and the World Bank decision last February, to put up the foreign-currency costs of this dam.

The United States offered an immediate grant of $56 million and Britain $14 million, with promises of sympathetic consideration to the tune of another $130 million. The World Bank agreed to lend $200 million, to begin four years hence when the initial stages had been completed with the aid of United States and British grants.

Since these offers were made Egypt has been reported behind the anti-American riots in Jordan and later the ouster of Britain's General Glubb from his long command of the Jordanian Army. Egypt was said to be supporting the Greek Cypriotes in their fight on Britain and the Algerian rebels in their struggle against France.

Egyptian propaganda, apparently operating on lines parallel to those of the Soviet Union, has become so active in pro-Western Libya that Libyan authorities have had to step in to stop it. Egyptian radio broadcasts to the peoples in the interior of Africa have seemed to incite nationalist violence. Egyptian propaganda has appeared to be seeking to stir up Moslem Ethiopians against their pro-Western Emperor; and Egypt has busily stirred the anti-Israeli fires in the Arab world.

As the impact of these developments piled up in Washington it became more and more clear that the time had come to end the "Be nice to Nasser" phase of Mideast policy.

Ambassador Byroade has been reassigned to South Africa; and when Egyptian Ambassador Ahmed Hussein came to see Mr. Dulles . . . about the offered grant for the High Dam, he was told, "Sorry. We have changed our mind."

The State Department centered its explanations in the economic problem—the argument that Egypt probably couldn't pay the internal costs. For this there was ample evidence, since Egypt had generously mortgaged her cotton crop many years ahead in barter deals with Communist China and other Communist countries.

Add to these considerations the facts that the Senate Appropriations Committee boldly "instructed" Mr. Dulles not to finance the High Dam, that legislators from cotton states feared Egyptian competition and that some congressmen feared Zionist disapproval, and the reasons for dropping the financing project are clear.

Now the Administration is expected to try a "Get tough with Nasser" line. This might involve the United States' taking a full membership in the Baghdad pact. It will surely involve stronger words from Mr. Dulles and perhaps the President. . . .

What the Russians and Egyptians will do about the new situation is in doubt. There are plausible reports that Moscow's Foreign Minister Shepilov offered a $1.1 billion loan for the project, and also plausible reports that he said he would prefer to back industrial projects. The State Department prefers the latter report. It thinks the Russians have perceived the economic pitfalls of the project. But it could be whistling in the dark. . . .

To borrow one of the State Department's favorite words, the situation in the Middle East has now been distinctly exacerbated.

With no solution of his basic economic problem in sight, Premier Nasser might be more than ever tempted to exploit the Israeli issue as a unifying force at home as well as in the Arab world.

In Washington, the officials most closely associated with the problem are glum. Many of them think the High Dam should be built by Western interests regardless of all the considerations mentioned, because it is in the long-term interest of the free world that Egypt should cope successfully with her economic difficulties.

As matters stand, these observers say, the only gainers are the Russians. By meddling in the Middle East, they have frustrated construction of this great project by the West. That is a Communist gain. Now they may get an opportunity to do the job themselves, thereby tying the Egyptian economy firmly to Russia.

That would be an even greater Communist gain.

BIBLIOGRAPHY

An asterisk (*) preceding a reference indicates that the article or a part of it has been reprinted in this book.

BIBLIOGRAPHIES

Ettinghausen, Richard, ed. A selected and annotated bibliography of books and periodicals in Western languages dealing with the Near and Middle East with special emphasis on medieval and modern times. 137p. With supplement, December 1953. The Middle East Institute. 1761 N St. Washington 6, D.C. '54.

Library Journal. 80:119-21. Ja. 15, '55. Bibliography on the Middle East, India and Pakistan. A. McCully.

Middle East Journal. Monthly bibliography of periodical literature on the Middle East. Sidney Glazer, comp.

BOOKS AND PAMPHLETS

Anshen, R. N. ed. Mid-East; world-center. 386p. Harper & Bros. New York. '56.

Antonius, George. Arab awakening; the story of the Arab national movement. 471p. J. B. Lippincott Co. Philadelphia. '39.

Awad, M. M. Challenge to the Arabs. 120p. Pageant Press. New York. '54.

Badeau, J. S. and Nolte, R. H. Emergence of modern Egypt. (Headline Series 98) 62p. Foreign Policy Association. New York. '53.

Baehr, Karl. Arab and Jewish refugees—problems and prospects. 12p. American Christian Palestine Committee. 471 Park Ave. New York 22. '53.

Ben-Gurion, David. Rebirth and destiny of Israel. 539p. Philosophical Library. New York. '53.

Brookings Institution. Security of the Middle East: a problem paper. 66p. The Institution. Washington, D.C. '50.

Byroade, H. A. Middle East. (Publication 5469) 28p. Public Services Division, Department of State. Washington 25, D.C. '54.

Cooke, H. V. Challenge and response in the Middle East. 366p. Harper & Bros. New York. '52.

Coon, C. S. Caravan; the story of the Middle East. 376p. Henry Holt & Co. New York. '51.

Douglas, W. O. Strange lands and friendly people. 336p. Harper & Bros. New York. '51.

Dulles, J. F. Middle East; address. (State Dept. Series S, no38) 6p. Public Services Division, Department of State. Washington 25, D.C. '55.

Eban, Abba. Egypt-Israel relations. 26p. Israel Office of Information. 11 E. 70th St. New York 21. '55.

Eban, Abba. Egypt's blockade practices in the Suez Canal and the Gulf of Aqaba. 32p. Israel Office of Information. 11 E. 70th St. New York 21. '54.

Eban, Abba. Security situation in the Middle East; full text of a statement made by Ambassador Eban before the Security Council of the United Nations, November 12, 1953. 50p. Israel Office of Information. 11 E. 70th St. New York 21. '53.

Fernau, F. W. Moslems on the march. 294p. Robert Hale. London. '55.

Fisher, Sidney and others. Social forces in the Middle East. 262p. Cornell University Press. Ithaca, N.Y. '55.

Fisher, W. B. Middle East: a physical, social and regional geography. 514p. E. P. Dutton & Co. New York. '50.

Frye, R. N. ed. Near East and the great powers. 214p. Harvard University Press. Cambridge, Mass. '51.

Hindus, Maurice. In search of a future; Persia, Egypt, Iraq, and Palestine. 270p. Doubleday and Co. New York. '49.

Hitti, P. K. History of the Arabs. 5th ed. rev. 882p. Macmillan Co. New York. '52.

Hoskins, H. L. Middle East: problem area in world politics. 311p. Macmillan Co. New York. '54.

Hurewitz, J. C. Middle East dilemmas. 273p. Harper & Bros. New York. '53.

Hurewitz, J. C. Struggle for Palestine. 404p. W. W. Norton & Co. New York. '50.

Huxley, Julian. From an antique land; ancient and modern in the Middle East. 310p. Crown Publishers. New York. '54.

Israel Office of Information. Arab refugees. 45p. The Office. 11 E. 70th St. New York 21. '53.

Israel Office of information. Arabs in Israel. 92p. The Office. 11 E. 70th St. New York 21. '55.

Israel Office of Information. Jerusalem and the United Nations. 31p. The Office. 11 E. 70th St. New York 21. '55.

Jackh, Ernest, ed. Background of the Middle East. 236p. Cornell University Press. Ithaca, N.Y. '52.

Jarvis, H. W. Pharaoh to Farouk. 387p. Macmillan Co. New York. '56.

Kirk, G. F. Middle East 1945-1950. 338p. (Issued under the auspices of the Royal Institute of International Affairs) Oxford University Press. New York. '54.

*Laqueur, W. Z. Communism and nationalism in the Middle East. 349p. Frederick Praeger Co. New York. '56.

Latham, Edward. Crisis in the Middle East. (Reference Shelf. v24, no2) 189p. H. W. Wilson Co. New York. '52.

Lenczowski, George. Middle East in world affairs. 459p. Cornell University Press. Ithaca, N.Y. '52.

Lengyel, Emil. Middle East today. (Discussion Series no2) 63p. Foreign Policy Association. New York. '54.

Lengyel, Emil. World without end: the Middle East. 374p. John Day Co. New York. '53.

Longrigg, S. H. Oil in the Middle East. 305p. (Issued under the auspices of the Royal Institute of International Affairs) Oxford University Press. New York. '54.

Malik, Charles. Trouble in Palestine—the Arab position; interview. 5p. Social Science Foundation, University of Denver. Denver, Colo. '54.

Middle East Institute. Americans and the Middle East: partners in the next decade; series of addresses and panel discussions at Fourth Annual Conference on Middle East Affairs, March 17-18, 1950. 63p. The Institute. 1761 N St. Washington 6, D.C. '50.

Middle East Institute. Islam in the modern world; series of addresses presented at the Fifth Annual Conference on Middle East Affairs, March 9-10, 1951. 76p. The Institute. 1761 N St. Washington 6, D.C. '51.

Morrison, S. A. Middle East tensions: political, social and religious. 198p. Harper & Bros. New York. '54.

Naguib, Mohammed. Egypt's destiny. 256p. Doubleday and Co. New York. '55.

Nasser, G. A. Egypt's liberation. 119p. Public Affairs Press. Washington, D.C. '55.

*Polk, W. R. and Butler, W. J. What the Arabs think. (Headline Series no96) 63p. Foreign Policy Association. New York. '52.

Royal Institute of International Affairs. Great Britain and Palestine, 1915-1945. (Information Paper no20) 177p. The Institute. London. '46.

Royal Institute of International Affairs. Middle East. 2d ed. 590p. Oxford University Press. New York. '54.

Sayegh, F. A. Border incidents: a background analysis. 13p. Arab Information Center. 445 Park Ave. New York 22. '55.

Sharett, Moshe and Eban, Abba. Toward security in the Middle East; statements. 15p. Israel Office of Information. 11 E. 70th St. New York 21. '55.

Shwadran, Benjamin. Middle East, oil and the Great Powers. 445p. Frederick Praeger Co. New York. '55.

Speiser, E. A. United States and the Near East. 283p. Harvard University Press. Cambridge, Mass. '50.

Thomas, L. V. and Frye, R. N. United States and Turkey and Iran. 291p. Harvard University Press. Cambridge, Mass. '51.

United Nations. Economic developments in the Middle East, 1945 to 1954. 236p. Columbia University Press. New York. '55.

United Nations Relief and Works Agency for Palestine Refugees in the Near East. Annual report of the director, covering the period 1 July 1954 to 30 June 1955. Columbia University Press. New York. '55.

United States. Department of Defense. Armed Forces Talk. (no458) 15p. Supt. of Docs. Washington 25, D.C. '53.

United States. Department of State. Israel. (Publication 5674, Near and Middle Eastern Series 17) 20p. Supt. of Docs. Washington 25, D.C. '54.

United States. Department of State. Jordan. (Publication 5907, Near and Middle Eastern Series 19) 11p. Supt. of Docs. Washington 25, D.C. '55.

United States. Department of State. Middle East; address by Secretary Dulles. (Series S, no38) The Department. Washington 25, D.C.

United States. Department of State. Middle East; address by H. A. Byroade. (Middle East Series 16) The Department. Washington 25, D.C. '54.

United States. Department of State. U.S. Policy in the Near East, South Asia, and Africa—1955. (Publication 6330, Near and Middle Eastern Series 20) 63p. Supt. of Docs. Washington 25, D.C. '56.

*United States. House of Representatives. Foreign Affairs Committee. Arab refugees and other problems in the Near East. (House Report no 1250) 23p. Supt. of Docs. Washington 25, D.C. '54.

Voss, C. H. Palestine problem today: Israel and its neighbors. 64p. Beacon Press. Boston. '53.

Warriner, Doreen. Land and poverty in the Middle East. 149p. Chatham House. London. '48.

PERIODICALS

Academy of Political Science. Proceedings. 24:443-66. Ja. '52. Impact of the West on Middle Eastern social institutions. C. S. Coon.

America. 94:59. O. 15, '55. Egypt looks to the Reds.

America. 94:120. O. 29, '55. Iran takes sides: Iraq-Turkey-Pakistan alliance.

America. 94:550. F. 18, '56. Oil: key to the Middle East.

America. 95:125. My. 5, '56. Middle East tightrope. V. S. Kearney.

American Economic Review. 45:58-73. My. '55. Investment in agriculture in underdeveloped countries (a case study of Turkey) W. H. Nichols.

American Mercury. 80:78-82. Mr. '55. Jews, Arabs and Zionism. L. J. Rosenwald.

American Mercury. 82:111-17. Ja. '56. Arab world awakens. F. A. Sayegh.

Annals of the American Academy of Political and Social Science. 288:47-
55. Jl. '53. Middle East power vacuum. Emil Lengyel.
*Annals of the American Academy of Political and Social Science. 294:
138-46. Jl. '54. Quest for security in the Middle East. H. L.
Hoskins.
Annals of the American Academy of Political and Social Science. 294:
147-50. Jl. '54. Arab commonwealth. A. M. Rifa'i.
Annals of the American Academy of Political and Social Science. 294:
151-7. Jl. '54. The United States in the changing Middle East.
N. S. Fatemi.
Atlantic Monthly. 195:16-19. My. '55. Atlantic report on the world
today.
Atlantic Monthly. 197:12+. F. '56. Turkey; Atlantic report on the
world today.
Business Week. p 100-4. Ap. 2, '55. Keeping the Reds out of the
Middle East.
Business Week. p 112-13+. Ja. 21, '56. West gropes to stave off Mid-
East peril.
*Business Week. p 176. F. 11, '56. For peace in the Middle East.
*Business Week. p 160. Ap. 21, '56. Western oil interests get caught
in the crossfire.
Catholic World. 180:334-41. F. '55. Danger spot of the world; our
Middle Eastern responsibility. R. E. Freeman.
Christian Century. 72:1011. S. 7, '55. American and British offer aid to
end Palestine warfare.
Christian Century. 72:1075. S. 21, '55. Propose U.S. guarantee of
Israel's borders.
Christian Century. 73:35. Ja. 11, '56. World focuses on the Middle
East.
Christian Century. 73:164. F. 8, '56. What will an Islamic state look
like?
Christian Century. 73:260-1. F. 29, '56. Rivalry for oil now comes into
open.
Collier's. 133:34-6+. Je. 25, '54. New frontier for freedom. E. A.
Mowrer.
Commentary. 20:435-9. N. '55. Soviet expansion into the Middle East.
George Lichtheim.
Commentary. 21:33-40. Ja. '56. Nationalism, revolution, and fantasy
in Egypt. George Lichtheim.
Commentary. 21:401-8. My. '56. Western self-interest and Israeli self-
defense. H. L. Lehrman.
Current History. 30:321-63. Je. '56. Report on the Middle East.
Economist. 176:137-8. Je. 9, '55. Perplexities in Israel.
Economist. 175:1109-11. Je. 25, '55. Orphan island.
Economist. 176:46. Jl. 2, '55. Turkish prospect.

Economist. 176:sup 1-16. Jl. 2, '55. Oil and social change in the Middle East.

Editorial Research Reports. 1, no 14: Ap. 13, '55. Middle East conflicts. W. T. Stone.

*Editorial Research Reports. 1, no 18:335-43. My. 9, '56. Middle East commitments. W. T. Stone.

Far Eastern Survey. 24:161-5. N. '55. New phase in Pakistan politics. S. O. Maron.

Foreign Affairs. 34:271-86. Ja. '56. Defense of the Near East. D. A. Rustow.

Foreign Policy Bulletin. 34:97-8+. Mr. 15, '55. Turkish democracy at crossroads. H. A. Reed.

Foreign Policy Bulletin. 34:105-6. Ap. 1, '55. Arabs want justice in Palestine. R. P. Johnson.

Foreign Policy Bulletin. 34:113-14. Ap. 15, '55. How the West looks to the Middle East. Mario Rossi.

Foreign Policy Bulletin. 35:6-8. S. 15, '55. Unwanted war: Israel and the Arabs. V. M. Dean.

Foreign Policy Bulletin. 35:9-11+. O. 1, '55. Israel and Egypt: two enemies, same goals. V. M. Dean.

Foreign Policy Bulletin. 35:22-4. O. 15, '55. Egypt: nation in search of personality. V. M. Dean.

*Foreign Policy Bulletin. 35:84-6. F. 15, '56. Should the U.S. sell arms to Israel? J. K. Javits; Mather Eliot.

*Foreign Policy Bulletin. 35:105-6. Ap. 1, '56. Cyprus: defense vs. nationalism. Mario Rossi.

Foreign Policy Bulletin. 35:107. Ap. 1, '56. Will Middle East blow up? Neal Stanford.

Fortune. 50:124-5+. O. '54. Churning in Middle East oil.

Fortune. 51:78. Ja. '55. State of Israel.

Harper's Magazine. 206:63-70. Ap. '53. Defense of the Middle East. B. H. Liddell Hart.

Harper's Magazine. 210:68-72. Mr. '55. Israel's policy of reprisals.
    Discussion. 210:6. My. '55.

International Affairs. 30:1-12. Ja. '54. Communism and Islam. Bernard Lewis.

International Conciliation. 506:225-83. Ja. '56. Jordan river valley. G. G. Stevens.

Life. 39:122-8+. N. 14, '55. Egypt's premier reveals how he made Red arms deal. Keith Wheeler.

Life. 40:42. Mr. 19, '56. Israel is here to stay.

Life. 40:20-7. Mr. 27, '56. Trouble in the East plagues the West.

Look. 17:38-40+. Ag. 11, '53. No peace for Israel. A. E. Stevenson.

Middle East Journal. 9:17-27. Winter '55. Appeal of communism in the Middle East. W. Z. Laqueur.

Middle East Journal. 9:163-6. Spring '55. Iraqi-Turkish pact.

Middle East Journal. 9:323-7. Summer '55. Economic problems in the Gaza strip. James Baster.

Middle East Journal. 9:373-84. Fall '55. Role in search of a hero. J. S. Badeau.

Middle East Journal. 9:397-412. Fall '55. Development of the Jordan valley waters. Don Peretz.

Middle East Journal. 9:434-5. Fall '55. Egyptian arms agreement (to buy arms from Czechoslovakia).

Middle Eastern Affairs. 6:1-12. Ja. '55. Prospects for a solution of the Jordan river valley dispute. D. A. Schmidt.

*Middle Eastern Affairs. 6:65-77. Mr. '55. Ten years of the Arab League. J. S. Raleigh.

*Middle Eastern Affairs. 6:101-8. Ap. '55. Democracy in the Middle East—its state and prospects. Bernard Lewis.

Middle Eastern Affairs. 6:129-30. Ap. '55. Iraq—economic survey (abstract).

Middle Eastern Affairs. 6:160-5. My. '55. Special agreement between the United Kingdom and Iraq.

Middle Eastern Affairs. 6:177-84. Je. '55. West and the defense of the Middle East. J. S. Raleigh.

*Middle Eastern Affairs. 6:337-44. N. '55. Soviet policy in the Middle East. D. J. Dallin.

Middle Eastern Affairs. 6:345. N. '55. Soviet note protesting Iran's adherence to the Turkish-Iraqi-Pakistan alliance, October 12, 1955.

Middle Eastern Affairs. 6:347-8. N. '55. Egyptian-Syrian defense pact, October 20, 1955; text.

Middle Eastern Affairs. 6:373-82. D. '55. Facts versus pacts. Moshe Perlmann.

*Nation. 181:431-6. N. 19, '55. War in the Middle East. Lillie Shultz; Jon Kimche.
        Reprinted in this book: Part I: Russia's lethal giveaway. Lillie Shultz. p431-5.

Nation. 182:65-6. Ja. 28, '56. NATO's shaky bastion. Geoffrey Lewis.

Nation. 182:152-4. F. 25, '56. Pipeline to disaster. Jon Kimche.

Nation. 182:192-3. Mr. 10, '56. Nasser of Egypt. Egon Kaskeline.

New Republic. 134:9-12. Ja. 30, '56. Dry tinder in the Middle East. Michael Straight.

New Republic. 134:14-16. Mr. 19, '56. Military illusions. H. J. Morgenthau.

New Republic. 134:44-6. Je. 11, '56. Courtship of the Arabs. W. Z. Laqueur.

*New York Times. p E5. N. 27, '55. Baghdad Pact completes long chain of defenses. Kennett Love.

*New York Times. p E5. Ja. 8, '56. Britain seeks way out of Middle East crisis. Benjamin Welles.

*New York Times. p E 10. Mr. 11, '56. Dangerous oversight in American policy. James Reston.

*New York Times. p9. Mr. 18, '56. Middle East reexamined; letter. J. P. Warburg.

*New York Times. p E5. Ap. 1, '56. U.S. and Britain at odds on the Middle East. D. A. Schmidt.

*New York Times. p 1+. Ap. 4, '56. Precise U.S. policy asked in Mideast. S. P. Brewer.

*New York Times. p30. Ap. 17, '56. For a Middle East policy; letter. W. R. Rees-Davies.

*New York Times. p E4. My. 6, '56. Waters of the Jordan: key issue in Mideast. Homer Bigart.

*New York Times. p 18. My. 19, '56. There is no drift to peace in Palestine. C. L. Sulzberger.

*New York Times. p 18. Je. 2, '56. The truth about Palestine.

*New York Times. p E3. Je. 10, '56. UN Secretary renews Mideast peace moves. T. J. Hamilton.

*New York Times. p E5. Jl. 8, '56. Palestine chronology: 1947-1956.

*New York Times. p E3. Jl. 22, '56. Aswan decision marks a turn in U.S. policy. James Reston.

*New York Times. p E5. Jl. 29, '56. Suez vital link in world trade. H. W. Baldwin.

*New York Times. p E5. Jl. 29, '56. Nasser's bold plans link canal and dam. Osgood Caruthers.

*New York Times. p E2. Ag. 26, '56. News of the week in review; the world.

New York Times Magazine. p9+. Je. 7, '53. Pink communism in the Middle East. Elizabeth Monroe.

*New York Times Magazine. p 13+. Ag. 30, '53. Key force in the Middle East: the mob. Elizabeth Monroe.

New York Times Magazine. p 11+. S. 18, '55. Israel and Egypt: myths and realities. Kennett Love and Harry Gilroy.

Newsweek. 45:67-8. F. 14, '55. Young ruler to watch.

Newsweek. 45:51-3. F. 28, '55. Remaking the Garden of Eden.

Newsweek. 45:48. Ap. 11, '55. 10,000 at the border.

Newsweek. 45:48. Ap. 18 '55. Asian friend of ours. E. K. Lindley.

Newsweek. 45:80-2. Je. 13, '55. Middle East today: oil and ferment.

Newsweek. 46:34-5+. Jl. 4, '55. Mideast: we lose the initiative. H. F. Kern.

Newsweek. 46:56. O. 17, '55. Behind Egypt's deal: Cotton for guns.

Newsweek. 46:48. O. 24, '55. Tension in the Middle East; an appraisal.

Newsweek. 47:42. F. 6, '56. Ben-Gurion offers new peace plan through Newsweek.

Newsweek. 47:38. F. 13, '56. Egypt's Nasser gives Arab peace plan through Newsweek.

Political Quarterly. 26:380-8. O. '55. State and religion in Israel. E. H. Samuel.

Political Quarterly. 26:323-35. D. '55. Turkey today. A. H. Hanson.

Reader's Digest. 66:83-8. Ap. '55. Inside Egypt. John Gunther.

Reporter. 13:23-9. N. 3, '55. Egypt's liberation province, the beginning of a beginning. Martin Flavin.

Reporter. 13:18-20. D. 1, '55. Saudi Arabia: oil, sand and royalties. Ray Alan.

Reporter. 13:11-16. D. 15, '55; 14:7. Ja. 12, '56. Report from Egypt and Israel. Claire Sterling.

Reporter. 13:20-2. D. 15, '55. Trouble on the northern tier. Ray Alan.

Reporter. 14:29-34. Ja. 26, '56. Miscalculation in Jordan. Hal Lehrman.

Saturday Evening Post. 227:26-7+. Mr. 19, '55. Island everyone wants. George Weller.

Saturday Evening Post. 228:28-9. S. 3, '55. Can we hold back the red tide? E. D. Hauser.

Scholastic. 66:17. Mr. 2, '55. Jordan power project.

Scholastic. 66:21. Mr. 16, '55. Trouble in the Holy Land.

Scholastic. 67:29. O. 27, '55. Iran turns to the West; joins Middle Eastern defensive alliance.

Scholastic. 67:29. O. 27, '55. Soviet-Egypt arms deal.

Scholastic. 67:25-31. D. 8, '55. Suez story.

Time. 64:23. Jl. 5, '54. Balance sheet; U.N. survey.

Time. 65:38. Mr. 7, '55. Strength for the northern tier; Turkish-Iraqi treaty.

Time. 65:42. Ap. 18, '55. Bold Shah.

Time. 65:35. Je. 13, '55. Unrest in the desert; Palestinian Arabs deported from Saudi Arabia.

*Time. 66:24-5. O. 24, '55. Turkey: a friend in trouble.

Time. 66:33-4. D. 5, '55. Baghdad bastion.

Time. 67:28-9. Mr. 12, '56. Passing of the proconsul.

Time. 67:29. Mr. 12, '56. Communist penetration.

U.S. News & World Report. 36:39-42. Mr. 12, '54. The United States closes a gap in Asia.

U.S. News & World Report. 38:115-17. Mr. 25, '55. Memo from Israel; people in arms.

U.S. News & World Report. 38:68-9. Je. 10, '55. What Russians are up to now; interview. F. R. Zorlu.

U.S. News & World Report. 39:22-4. S. 2, '55. Threats to U.S. overseas bases.

*U.S. News & World Report. 39:48-52+. N. 4, '55. Where war threatens now; interviews. G. A. Nasser; Moshe Sharett.

U.S. News & World Report. 40:24-5. Mr. 2, '56. Why Saudi Arabia got those tanks.

U.S. News & World Report. 40:70-4. Mr. 16, '56. Boy king defies the British.

U.S. News & World Report. 40:26-30+. Mr. 23, '56. What they all mean: Mediterranean crisis.

U.S. News & World Report. 40:112-14. Mr. 23, '56. Why an archbishop was banished from Cyprus; text of a statement by the British Government.

United Nations Bulletin. 14:298-9. Ap. 15, '53. Middle East economies making slow progress.

United Nations Review. 2:38-9+. Ag. '55. Progress in economies of the Middle East.

United Nations Review. 2:38-41. O. '55. Council resolution on separating forces of Egypt and Israel.

United States Department of State Bulletin. 30:444-8. Mr. 22, '54. Middle East and south Asia, the problem of security; address, March 7, 1954. J. D. Jernegan.

United States Department of State Bulletin. 30:628-33. Ap. 26, '54. Middle East in new perspective. H. A. Byroade.

United States Department of State Bulletin. 30:708-13. My. 10, '54. Facing realities in the Arab-Israel dispute; address, May 1, 1954. H. A. Byroade.
  Same. Vital Speeches of the Day. 20:498-503. Je. 1, '54.

United States Department of State Bulletin. 31:6-8. Jl. 5, '54. Twentieth century comes to the Arabian peninsula. R. H. Sanger.

United States Department of State Bulletin. 31:230-3. Ag. 16, '54. Agreement between Iran and international oil consortium; messages and statements concerning the agreement.

United States Department of State Bulletin. 31:985-6. D. 27, '54. Arrangements for participation in Iranian oil consortium.

United States Department of State Bulletin. 32:301-6. F. 21, '55. Development of United States policy in the Near East, south Asia, and Africa during 1954. H. N. Howard.

*United States Department of State Bulletin. 32:564-9. Ap. 4, '55. Middle East defense; address, March 5, 1955. J. D. Jernegan.

United States Department of State Bulletin. 32:654. Ap. 18, '55. $20 million loan to Pakistan for defense support.

United States Department of State Bulletin. 32:659-63. Ap. 18, '55. Egyptian-Israeli dispute before the Security Council.

*United States Department of State Bulletin. 32:760-6. My. 9, '55. Social discontent in the Near East: a challenge to public responsibility. S. P. Dorsey.

United States Department of State Bulletin. 33:458-9. S. 19, '55. Essential objectives for maintenance of peace in the Near East; statement with text of resolution. H. C. Lodge, Jr.

United States Department of State Bulletin. 33:604-5. O. 17, '55. Transcript of Secretary Dulles' news conference, October 4, 1955.

United States Department of State Bulletin. 33:683-6. O. 31, '55. U.S. policy in the Middle East; address, October 17, 1955. G. V. Allen.

United States Department of State Bulletin. 33:926. D. 5, '55. U.S. support for the Baghdad Pact; statement. Waldemar Gallman.

United States Department of State Bulletin. 34:16-18. Ja. 2, '56. Baghdad Pact council concludes first meeting.

United States Department of State Bulletin. 34:506-9. Mr. 26, '56. Elements of hope in the Middle East economic picture; address, March 10, 1956. C. H. Seager.

United States Department of State Bulletin. 34:875-9. My. 28, '56. Mutual security program for the Near East, South Asia, and Africa. G. V. Allen.

University of Chicago Round Table. no784:1-16. Moslem world and the West. G. E. von Grunebaum and others. '53.

University of Chicago Round Table. no845:1-16. Changing Middle East. Z. N. Mahmoud and others. '54.

Vital Speeches of the Day. 19:613-14. Ag. 1, '53. Israel and the Arab nations. Abba Eban.

Vital Speeches of the Day. 20:200-5. Ja. 15, '54. Significance of the Suez Canal in current international affairs. J. S. Badeau.

Vital Speeches of the Day. 20:295-300. Mr. 1, '54. Middle East problem. Dorothy Thompson.

Vital Speeches of the Day. 21:1256-8. Je. 1, '55. Address at Asian-African conference. G. A. Nasser.

Vital Speeches of the Day. 22:173-7. Ja. 1, '56. Who is winning in the Middle East? M. F. Jamali.

World Today. 11:145-51. Ap. '55. Iraq, Egypt, and the Arab League.

World Today. 11:238-45. Je. '55. Israel after seven lean years.

World Today. 11:415-17. O. '55. Some wider aspects of the Cyprus problem.